dr. richter's
healthy living
seafood guide

Shrimp & Vegetable Kabobs, see page 75

For Cover Recipe, Baked Orange Roughy with Dill, see page 61.

Try-Foods International, Inc.
207 Semoran Commerce Place
Apopka, Florida 32703
Printed in the United States of America
To reorder call 1-800-421-8871

foreword

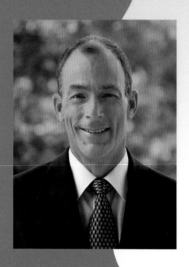

Seafood is wonderful. It is versatile. You may grill it—my favorite. You may bake it or add it to soup. There are dozens of regional ways to prepare seafood—grilled salmon from the Pacific Northwest, boiled lobster from Maine, planked whitefish from the Great Lakes region or Jambalaya from New Orleans. Healthy seafood entices diners everywhere with a meal full of flavor and texture.

Seafood is good for you. I, along with other medical authorities and registered dietitians, recommend you serve it to your family at least twice a week. The nutrients in seafood may amaze you. For instance, a serving of oysters contains over 500% of the daily requirement for vitamin B12 and more than 200% of your daily zinc needs. Shrimp, America's favorite seafood, supplies plentiful vitamin B12, iron and zinc.

Seafood is a healthy way to satisfy your family's protein needs. Fats found in fish are mainly unsaturated. These fats, especially the monounsaturated fats, help lower blood cholesterol levels. The "fattiest" fish—salmon, tuna and other cold water fish—provide a special type of polyunsaturated fat named omega-3 fatty acids. These nutrients help lower bad cholesterol levels, stabilize the heart rhythm, and prevent dangerous blood clots from forming.

This book is a complete guide to preparing healthy seafood for your family. Learn how to buy it, the importance of keeping it fresh and several preferred cooking methods. Along with culinary experts, I've included more than 60 healthy recipes perfect for seafood lovers or those just learning to experience the delights of this nutritious food.

Read on, keep this reference handy in the kitchen and join me in enjoying the wonders of serving seafood!

H J Richter

Henry J. Richter, MD, FACEP

table of contents

foreword   2

seafood's contribution
to healthy eating   4

nutrition chart   7

flavor chart   8

buying seafood   9

quick easy tips to keep
your seafood safe at home   10

cleaning fish   12

filleting fish   12

raw seafood   13

methyl mercury in seafood   13

environmental concerns   13

cooking fish   14

hot grill tips   16

how to shuck a clam   27

how to crack a cooked
hard-shell crab   39

how to crack a
cooked lobster   53

how to peel & devein
shrimp   81

glossary   92

index   94

species & recipes

catfish   20

clams   24

cod   28

crab   32

flounder   40

grouper   42

haddock   44

halibut   48

lobster   50

mackerel   54

mahi mahi   56

ocean perch   58

orange roughy   60

salmon   64

scallops   70

sea bass   72

shrimp   74

snapper   82

tilapia   84

trout   86

tuna   88

seafood's contribution

*F*inally, a tasty food that experts encourage you to eat! Abundant in vitamins and minerals, seafood contains lots of protein and minimal fat, making it low in calories and good for you.

Fish are excellent sources of essential minerals, including potassium, iron, phosphorus, copper, iodine, cobalt and selenium. Some types of shellfish also provide health-promoting zinc and calcium. Seafood's natural diet produces a high mineral content. Ocean grazers, such as shrimp, eat the vegetables of the sea—seaweed, kelp and algae—that concentrate minerals from sea water, while larger fish eat the shrimp. Whether fish or shellfish, a seafood supper is an easy way for you to get the benefits of minerals in your diet. Even though minerals compose only 4% of your body weight, they're essential for regulating fluid balance, muscle contractions, and nerve impulses. Minerals also give structure to your bones, teeth, muscles, blood and other body tissues.

to healthy eating

Vitamins abound in all seafood. Fish contain large amounts of B-complex vitamins that produce energy in your body. Fatty fish, such as salmon and tuna, are good sources of vitamins A and D. Vitamin A promotes the growth and health of cells and protects you against infection. Vitamin D helps your body absorb minerals and regulates blood calcium levels. Herring and mackerel add vitamin E to your diet. Vitamin E works as an antioxidant, possibly lowering the risk for heart disease and stroke.

Seafood has less total fat and less saturated fat than meat or poultry. Except for some shellfish, seafood is also low in cholesterol. The triple benefit of low fat, low saturated fat, and low cholesterol make seafood a good choice. Even shrimp and crayfish, which have higher cholesterol levels than other seafood, are low in fat and saturated fat, making them heart-healthy choices.

All seafood supplies healthy doses of omega-3 fatty acids—polyunsaturated fatty acids with special structures that provide benefits beyond basic nutrition. Although these advantageous fatty acids are found in a few other foods (certain oils, nuts and seeds), fish are the primary dietary source. Seafood coming from cold waters— mackerel, albacore tuna, Atlantic herring, swordfish, lake trout, salmon, sea bass, oysters, mussels and sardines—contain the greatest amounts of omega-3 fatty acids.

the omega-3 advantage

Nutritionists continue to document the health benefits associated with omega-3 fatty acids. These fatty acids play a role in reducing heart disease, lowering blood pressure and decreasing cholesterol levels. They help prevent cardiac arrhythmias, which cause virtually all cases of sudden death. They work by thinning blood and reducing blood platelet clotting, lowering the risk for blocked blood vessels and heart attack. They also relax arteries, improving blood circulation. Other benefits associated with omega-3 fatty acids may include alleviating the symptoms of rheumatoid arthritis, improving insulin function, assisting in eye and brain development of infants and possibly easing depression.

Even with the amazing powers of omega-3 fatty acids, they are not a magical remedy for heart disease. You can't simply pop a fish-oil capsule and expect it to undo the effects of a high-fat, high-calorie diet. Instead, substitute grilled, baked, poached or broiled fish for more fat-laden beef, pork or poultry twice weekly. This will provide the benefits of omega-3 fatty acids and reduce your calorie intake, lowering your risk for diabetes, heart disease and some cancers.

SEAFOOD	Calories Kilojoules	Protein (g)	Fat (g)	Cholesterol (mg)	Sodium (mg)	Iron (mg)	Potassium (mg)
er 3 oz. (85 grams) Cooked*		(g)	(g)	(mg)	(mg)	(mg)	(mg)
altwater Fish							
Cod							
Atlantic Cod	89 / 373	19.41	0.73	46.34	66.30	0.42	207.40
Pacific Cod	89 / 373	19.51	0.69	39.95	77.35	0.28	439.45
Flounder (mixed species)	99 / 417	20.54	1.30	57.80	89.25	0.29	292.40
Grouper	100 / 420	21.11	1.10	39.95	45.05	0.97	403.75
Haddock	95 / 339	20.60	0.79	62.90	73.95	1.15	339.15
Halibut	119 / 498	22.69	2.50	34.85	58.65	0.91	489.60
Mackerel							
Atlantic Mackerel	223 / 932	20.27	15.14	63.75	70.55	1.33	340.85
King Mackerel	114 / 477	22.10	2.18	57.80	172.55	1.94	474.30
Pacific Jack Mackerel	171 / 715	21.87	8.60	51.00	93.50	1.27	442.85
Ocean Perch							
Atlantic Ocean Perch	103 / 430	20.30	1.78	45.90	81.60	1.00	297.50
Pacific Ocean Perch	103 / 430	20.43	1.71	37.40	65.45	0.45	442.00
Orange Roughy	76 / 316	16.02	0.77	22.10	68.85	0.20	327.25
Pollock							
Atlantic Pollock	100 / 420	21.18	1.07	77.35	93.50	0.50	387.60
Alaskan Pollock	96 / 402	19.98	0.95	81.60	98.60	0.24	328.95
Salmon, Coho	151 / 633	20.65	7.00	53.55	44.20	0.33	391.00
Snapper (mixed species)	109 / 456	22.36	1.46	39.95	48.45	0.20	443.70
Sole (mixed species)	99 / 417	20.54	1.30	57.80	89.25	0.29	292.40
Tilapia	110 / 460	21.00	2.50	55.00	55.00	1.50	292.40
Tuna, Yellowfin	118 / 495	25.47	1.04	49.30	39.95	0.80	483.65
Whiting (mixed species)	99 / 412	19.96	1.44	71.40	112.20	0.36	368.90
reshwater Fish							
Catfish (channel)	129 / 541	15.91	6.82	54.40	68.00	0.70	272.85
Rainbow Trout	144 / 601	20.63	6.12	57.80	35.70	0.28	374.85
hellfish							
Clams (mixed species)	125 / 526	21.72	1.66	56.95	95.20	23.77	533.80
Lobster, Northern	83 / 349	17.42	0.50	61.20	323.00	0.33	299.20
Oysters							
Eastern & Gulf	116 / 487	11.99	4.17	89.25	358.70	10.19	238.85
Pacific	139 / 580	16.07	3.91	85.00	180.20	7.82	256.70
Scallops (mixed species)	183 / 765	15.37	9.30	51.88	394.63	0.70	283.22
Shrimp (mixed species)	84 / 352	17.77	0.92	165.75	190.40	2.63	154.70

The nutritional values in this chart are approximations.

chart your course

flavor

Seafood flavors vary with growing conditions. Factors such as water quality, water salinity, weather and harvest location all influence taste. Some of the same factors also affect availability. This chart divides fish and shellfish into groups by texture and flavor. Use it to find species that can be substituted in recipes when needed.

	MILD FLAVOR	MODERATE FLAVOR	FULL FLAVOR
Delicate Texture	Flounder Pollock Sole	Butterfish	Oysters
Moderate Texture	Drum Haddock Ocean Perch Orange Roughy Rockfish Salmon (Atlantic) Salmon (chum) Scallops Snapper Tilapia Trout Walleye Whitefish	Mullet Salmon (coho) Smelt	Salmon (Sockeye)
Firm Texture	Catfish Cod Crab Crawfish Croaker Grouper Halibut Mahi Mahi Marlin Sea Bass Shark Sheepshead Shrimp Sturgeon Whiting	Amberjack Clams Lake Victoria Perch Lobster Monkfish Pompano Tuna	Mackerel Mussels Swordfish

Finding freshness is important when shopping for seafood. Ask where seafood came from, when it was caught, how it was caught and how it was stored. Limit your purchases to reputable, commercial sources or to known vendors. When you walk into the market, rely on your senses. A well-kept fish market should smell like the sea, but not "fishy" and should not have a whiff of ammonia. Look for spotless floors, counters and display cases.

Judge fish by its aroma and appearance.
Look for:

- Shiny, taut skin that sparkles in the light. As fish deteriorates, its colors fade.
- Flesh that feels firm and will spring back when lightly pressed.
- Fillets and steaks with a moist, clean-cut appearance. Ragged edges or off color indicates poor quality.
- Scales that adhere tightly. Loose scales are a sign of improper handling.
- Bright and bulging, clear eyes (some fish, such as walleye, never have clear eyes). Don't purchase any fish with dull or sunken eyes.
- Gills that are bright red and not slippery. As fish loses quality the gills begin to fade.

Guidelines for buying shellfish:

- Purchase mussels and clams live. The shells of live mussels, clams and oysters may open naturally but will close when tapped, indicating that they are alive. Discard any dead ones. (Soft shell clams and geoducks always gape enough for the protruding siphon, however, the siphon will pull in when touched.)

- Shucked oysters and scallops should have a fresh, sweet aroma. Avoid any with a strong odor. 
- Live crabs and lobsters should be moving their legs and be active. Lobsters will curl their tails beneath them when they are picked up.
- Ask how long lobsters and crabs have been kept in a tank. If it's more than a week, reject them. Their texture and flavor deteriorate when stored for longer periods.

How Much to Buy

Deciding how much seafood to buy depends upon how you intend to prepare it and the desired size of individual servings. The quantities listed below are good portions for an adult entrée. Use smaller quantities for appetizers and casseroles where other ingredients are included.

Type of Seafood	Serving Per Person
Whole fish	½ to 1 pound (226 to 454g)
Fillets	¼ to ⅓ pound (113 to 151g)
Steaks	¼ to ½ pound (113 to 226g)
Live crab	1 pound (454g)
Live lobster	1 small to medium
Lobster meat	¼ to ⅓ pound (113 to 151g)
Lobster tail	½ pound (226g)
Oysters	half a dozen
Scallops	¼ to ⅓ pound (113 to 151g)
Shrimp, peeled	¼ to ⅓ pound (113 to 151g)
Shrimp, unpeeled	½ to ¾ pound (226 to 339g)

quick, easy tips

to keep your seafood safe at home

Fighting bacteria that cause foodborne illness is a key concern in the seafood market. What you do at home to prevent the spread of germs is equally important. Members of the food industry and various health organizations have joined together to educate consumers on four simple tasks to safeguard their food supply. The "Fight BAC!™" program targets what you should do: fight back to reduce the incidence of foodborne illness by following safe food handling practices. Log on to www.fightbac.org and find out more.

CLEAN

- Clean all preparation surfaces as well as hands, fingernails and exposed arms before and after handling raw seafood.
- Wash your hands with hot water and soap for 20 seconds.
- When wiping counters, cutting boards, utensils and hands, use a disposable paper towel.
- Use plastic (non-porous) cutting boards that can be run through the dishwasher. Keep a cutting board that you use only for raw meat and seafood. (Or, use a disposable cutting sheet and throw it out.)

SEPARATE

- To avoid cross-contamination, keep different types of seafood separate from each other and also from other grocery items.
- Keep raw seafood and sushi AWAY from other foods that are ready to eat.
- Beware of liquids from packages of seafood dripping onto other items in the grocery cart, grocery bag and refrigerator.
- Use different plates, utensils and cutting boards for preparing and serving foods. Wiping and rinsing them off between preparation and serving is not sufficient to kill bacteria.

COOK

Cook your seafood to recommended food temperatures. Proper cooking will kill most bacteria. Buy a small kitchen thermometer for at-home food safety.

Suggested Minimum Internal Cooking Temperatures
(Temperature to be maintained for at least 15 seconds)
- Solid portions of fish, shrimp and lobster 145°F/63°C
- Stuffed seafood 165°F/74°C

OTHER COOKING GUIDELINES:

- Raw shrimp in shells—Cook until pink and firm. Allow 3 to 5 minutes to boil or steam 1 pound (454g) of medium-size shrimp in their shells.

- Peeled shrimp—Cook until pink and firm. Boil for 1 to 3 minutes.

- Oysters, mussels and clams in the shell—Thoroughly scrub shells. Steam for 4 to 9 minutes or boil for 3 to 5 minutes after the shells open. Discard any that do not open.

- Shucked shellfish (clams, oysters and mussels without shells)—Cook until plump and opaque. Boil for 3 minutes, fry in oil at 375°F/191°C for 10 minutes or bake for 10 minutes at 450°F/232°C.

- Boiled lobster—Cook until shell is bright red; boil 5 to 6 minutes per pound (454g) after putting lobster in pot and water has returned to a boil.

- Scallops—Cook until milky white or opaque and firm. Depending on their size, allow about 3 to 4 minutes total cooking time.

- Hard-shell crabs—Cook until shells turn pink; simmer 10 minutes after putting about 3 pounds (1.36kg) of crabs in pot and water has returned to a boil.

CHILL

- Bring a small ice chest when grocery shopping if you have a long trip home or if it is a warm, sunny day.

- Refrigerate fish as close to 32°F/0°C as possible. Use within 24 hours.

- Refrigerate live mussels, oysters and clams in shells at about 35°F/2°C on a tray draped with a moist cloth for up to 2 days. Do not place on ice or allow fresh water to come in contact with them. Make sure they are still alive by tapping any open shells before cooking. If they do not close, throw them away.

- Shucked oysters, scallops and clams may be refrigerated in their own containers as close to 32°F/0°C as possible. Surround the containers with ice for best results.

- Refrigerate live crabs or lobsters in moist packaging such as seaweed or damp paper strips or drape with a moist cloth for up to 24 hours. Do not place them in airtight containers, water or salted water. Make sure they are still moving before cooking.

- Refrigerate fresh, peeled shrimp in a tightly covered container as close to 32°F/0°C as possible. Use within 2 days.

- Frozen seafood should be wrapped airtight and stored at 0°F/-18°C or below for no more than 6 months.

- Defrost and marinate seafood in the refrigerator. Defrost in the microwave, ONLY if you are going to cook the seafood right away. Never defrost or marinate seafood at room temperature.

- Refrigerate cooked seafood, tightly covered, for up to 2 days in the coldest part of your refrigerator.

- Don't keep seafood too long in the refrigerator or freezer. If in doubt, throw it out.

cleaning fish

M ost fish markets sell fish in several forms. They are:

Drawn (gutted fish with the head and fins intact)

Dressed (gutted and scaled fish with gills removed, often fins, too, are removed)

Pan-dressed (gutted and scaled fish with head and fins removed; tail is usually trimmed)

Fish steak (a crosscut slice from a large, dressed fish)

Fish fillet (a boneless piece of fish cut lengthwise from the side and away from the backbone of the fish)

If you purchase a whole fish, it's important to clean it as quickly as possible to prolong the shelf life. First remove the scales. Using a solid table top, hold the fish firmly with one hand. Make sure the fish doesn't slide as you work. With your other hand use a knife or scraper and work from tail to head to remove the scales.

Use a sharp knife to remove the fish's head. Cut from the top of the head down through the spine, cutting behind the gills on both sides of the fish. Pull the head down, removing the internal organs with the head. Discard the internal organs. Do not allow them to mix with the fish flesh.

Remove the top and bottom fins by grasping the fins with a pair of pliers and pulling toward the head end of the fish. Cut off the tail fin with a sharp knife. Thoroughly wash the fish under cold running water, making sure any blood, scales or internal organs are rinsed away. Place the fish in a clean pan.

FILLETING FISH

Start with a dressed fish or dress your own as described above. Use a well-sharpened knife to cut the meat as close to the spine and rib cage as possible by sliding the knife from the head end of the fish toward the tail. Repeat on the other side of the fish. You should have two fillets from one fish. Find any remaining fine bones by gently rubbing from the head end to the tail end with your fingertips. Remove the fine bones by pulling them out with clean tweezers.

If you want the skin removed, place the fillet skin-side down on a cutting board. Insert a sharp knife between the meat and skin at the tail end of the fillet. Firmly hold the skin and move the knife in a gently sawing motion to cut the meat away from the skin.

raw seafood

Many people enjoy eating sushi and seviche, which contain raw seafood. Although all raw seafood contains naturally occurring bacteria, it imposes minimal risks when carefully controlled. If you prepare raw fish at home, be sure to start with the highest-quality ingredients—VERY fresh and purchased from a known, licensed, reputable dealer. For clams, mussels and oysters ask to see the certified shipper's tag. Freeze the seafood at 0°F/-18°C or lower for 24 hours before you use it. If you are uncertain about the quality of seafood or the temperature at which you can keep it frozen, limit your sushi or seviche consumption to high-quality restaurants.

When you eat out, sushi, seviche and oyster bars are usually safe if they use sushi-grade or high-quality seafood. Select a reputable restaurant that buys seafood that meets safety and

sanitation standards and handles seafood safely.

There are certain people who should never eat raw or under cooked seafood. These at-risk groups have weakened immune systems that cannot effectively fight bacteria. They include people with liver disease; diabetes; cancer; immune disorders, including AIDS; chronic alcohol use; hemochromatosis (an iron disorder); gastrointestinal disorders; inflammatory bowel disease; steroid dependency; and kidney disease. Children, pregnant women and elderly persons should also avoid raw or under cooked seafood.

METHYL MERCURY IN SEAFOOD

Mercury is naturally present in soil, air, water and all living things. It finds its way into seafood when underwater volcanoes erupt or when mercury from the air falls into the water. Bacteria in the water changes mercury to methyl mercury, which is toxic. Over a period of time, methyl mercury buildup may occur in large, long-living fish, such as shark, swordfish, king mackerel, tilefish, tuna, pike, bass, halibut, grouper, snapper or walleye. For most people there is little risk of methyl mercury poisoning from commercially harvested fish. However, because mercury is a potential risk to developing nervous systems, pregnant women, women who might become pregnant and nursing mothers should avoid species of fish subject to buildups of methyl mercury. They can safely eat up to 8 to 12 ounces (226 to 340g) per week of other cooked fish, shellfish, canned fish, farm-raised fish, and small ocean fish. Young children should avoid all of the above except for canned tuna, and can safely eat up to 1.5 ounces (42.5g) per week.

ENVIRONMENTAL CONCERNS

News about the environment and the world's seas concerns many people. The atmosphere, climate and varied aquatic life comprise a complex ecosystem. Commercial fishing impacts this system in a number of ways. That's why international and regional organizations implement strict regulations that govern which species can be harvested, when, and how much. Regulations protect young fish and those most likely to breed. Other rules guard against overfishing or depleting supplies of species. According to the United Nations, 75% of the world's fisheries are being used at or below the level of sustainability. Laws protect the remaining 25% of the world's fisheries and techniques are implemented to restore those stocks.

Fish farming or aquaculture is good for the environment. Fish use available resources more efficiently than other animals. For example, seafood usually consume 1 to 2 pounds (454 to 907g) of feed for every pound (454g) of human food created. Beef cattle eat up to 7 pounds (3.18kg) of feed for every pound (454g) of meat created. Growing seafood results in less waste and pollution. Advances are also being made to limit the amount of chemicals used in fish farming.

cooking fish
10-minute rule

Minutes count when cooking fish. Cooked perfectly, fish will be moist and tender. Fish is done when it begins to flake easily with a fork and loses its translucent or raw appearance. A useful guideline is the 10-minute rule—allow 10 minutes for every inch (2.5cm) of thickness. Measure fish at its thickest part—if fish is stuffed or rolled, measure it after stuffing or rolling. Add 5 minutes to the total cooking time if you are cooking fish in foil or if the fish is cooked in a sauce. Double the cooking time (20 minutes per inch or 2.5cm) for frozen fish that has not been thawed. This handy 10-minute rule applies to baking, broiling, grilling, sautéing, steaming or poaching fillets, steaks or whole fish. (Do not apply the 10-minute rule when microwaving fish.)

BAKING

Place fish in a single layer in a greased shallow baking dish. For fillets, tuck under any thin portions. Season lightly with salt, pepper or herbs. Drizzle with a little melted butter. Bake, uncovered, at 450°F/232°C.

SAUTÉING OR PAN-FRYING

Lightly dredge the fish in seasoned flour, cornmeal or cracker crumbs. In a large skillet heat a little butter or olive oil until the pan is very hot. Add the fish and cook, turning once.

POACHING

Fill a large skillet with 2 to 3 inches (5 to 8cm) of water, broth or wine. Season with herbs, onion, lemon or peppercorns, if desired. Bring to a boil. Add fish fillet or steak. Return to a boil. Reduce heat so the liquid just simmers. Cover and begin timing. Leftover poaching liquid can be used to make a sauce, if desired.

BROILING

Preheat the broiler. Spray the rack of an unheated broiler pan with nonstick cooking spray or lightly grease the rack. Place fish fillets or steaks on the prepared broiler pan rack. For fillets, tuck under any thin portions. Broil about 4 inches (10cm) from the heat until done. Fish that's less than 1 inch (2.5cm) thick does not require turning. Fish 1 inch (2.5cm) thick or more should be turned once halfway through cooking.

STEAMING

Select a deep pot or steam cooker with a tight-fitting lid. Add a wire basket or rack to hold the fish. Fill the pot with water to within 1 to 2 inches (2.5 to 5cm) of the rack. Bring the water to boiling and gently place the fish on the rack. Reduce heat so the water gently boils. Cover the pot tightly and cook until done.

MICROWAVE COOKING

Do not use the 10-minute rule with microwave cooking. In a baking dish arrange fish fillets with any thicker portions toward the outside of the dish and thinner portions overlapping in the center of the dish. Sprinkle with herbs, if desired. Cover with vented plastic wrap. For a cooking guideline, calculate about 3 minutes per pound (454g) of boneless fish. Cook on 100% power (HIGH) until fish is done. Check fish when two-thirds of the time has elapsed.

hot grill tips

Fish and seafood grilled over hot coals or on a gas grill taste terrific. It's easy to do. Choose either direct or indirect grilling, depending on the shape and size of the food. Follow the directions on these pages and start the grill! In minutes you'll be serving fabulous fish or succulent seafood.

DIRECT HEAT (SIMILAR TO BROILING):

In direct heat cooking, food cooks directly over glowing charcoal or lit gas burners. Use direct heat for small whole fish, kabobs, fish fillets, fish steaks, or any food that cooks in 20 minutes or less. To prevent sticking, grease the grill basket, grill rack, or grill screen before starting. Fish fillets cook best in a grill basket or on a screen. Whole fish and steaks grill fine directly on the grill rack. Small pieces, such as cubes of fish, scallops or shrimp, need to be threaded on skewers or placed on a grill screen.

For charcoal grills, cook the food, uncovered, directly over medium coals. For gas grills, preheat the grill and then reduce the heat to medium. Add the fish or seafood, shut the cover, and grill directly over medium heat. Turn foods once halfway through the cooking time. Brush with any glazes or sauces during the last few minutes of grilling.

INDIRECT HEAT (SIMILAR TO ROASTING):

Indirect heat cooks more slowly and gently than direct heat, allowing you to cook large whole fish or thick fish fillets without burning them. A covered grill is required for indirect cooking.

When using indirect heat, set charcoal briquettes on the periphery of the firebox and

place the food on the center of the grill rack. Or, light gas burners on one side of the grill (or the front and back) and place the food over the unlit burners. You may want a drip pan beneath the food to catch fat drippings and minimize flare-ups; however, fish and seafood usually contain so little fat that a drip pan is not required. Place fish or seafood on a greased grill rack over medium heat. Ordinarily, medium-hot coals or a medium-hot gas setting is needed to produce a medium heat in the cooking area. Cover the grill and cook. There's no need to turn foods cooked with indirect heat.

COOKING TIMES:

Variables such as wind, outside air temperature, desired doneness, and the shape of fish or seafood affect cooking times. Use these timings as general guidelines and add or subtract time to accommodate your circumstances.

Fish is done when it flakes easily with a fork or when a meat thermometer inserted into the thickest portion of fish registers 145°F/63°C. Seafood is done when it turns opaque.

DIRECT GRILLING TIMES

FORM OF FISH	SIZE	APPROXIMATE TIME
Whole fish	½ to 1½ pounds (226 to 680g)	6 to 9 minutes per 8 ounces (226g)
Fillets, steaks	½ to 1 inch thick (1.3 to 2.5cm)	4 to 6 minutes per ½-inch (1.3cm) thickness
Lobster tails	6 ounces (170g) 8 ounces (226g)	6 to 10 minutes 12 to 15 minutes
Shrimp	20 per pound (454g) 12 to 15 per pound (454g)	5 to 8 minutes 7 to 9 minutes

INDIRECT GRILLING TIMES

FORM OF FISH	SIZE	APPROXIMATE TIME
Whole fish	2 to 4 pounds (907g to 1.8kg)	20 to 30 minutes per pound (454g)
Fillets, steaks	½ to 1½ inches (1.3 to 3.8cm)	7 to 9 minutes per ½-inch (1.3cm) thickness
Shrimp	20 per pound (454g) 12 to 15 per pound (454g)	8 to 10 minutes 9 to 11 minutes

HOW HOT IS HOT?

To test the temperature of your grill, hold your hand near the cooking level and count how many seconds you can leave it there before it becomes uncomfortable.

3 seconds . . . . medium-hot

4 seconds . . . . medium

5 seconds . . . . low

If the temperature is too hot, raise the grill rack, spread the coals, lower the gas setting, or remove some briquettes. If the temperature is too cool, knock ashes off the coals, add briquettes, lower the grill rack, or increase the gas setting.

STARTING A CHARCOAL FIRE

Use enough charcoal briquettes to cover an area on the bottom of the grill that is 3 to 4 inches (8 to 10cm) larger on all sides than the food to be grilled. If the weather is humid or windy, add a little extra charcoal. Group the briquettes into a mound and ignite. When the flame dies down and the coals turn gray (20 to 30 minutes), spread them in a single layer.

STARTING A GAS GRILL

Follow the manufacturer's directions.

SMOKING

For a smokier flavor, add water-soaked mesquite, cherry or apple wood chips to your grill. You can put drained chips directly on the hot coals in a charcoal grill. For gas grills, place the soaked chips and a little water in a foil pan alongside the food on the grill rack.

SEASONING

Add any of these seasonings to grilled seafood. They all taste great.

Dill weed	Tarragon
Allspice	Basil
Horseradish	Nutmeg
Chives	Garlic powder
Lemon or lime juice	White wine
Tarragon vinegar	

recipes

Crab Quesadillas with Papaya Sauce, see page 39

catfish

Catfish, also known as channel cats, are easily identified by the long whiskers called barbels.

SOURCE: Most catfish are farm-raised in Mississippi, Alabama, Arkansas or Louisiana. Catfish ponds are built over clay-rich soil, filled with fresh water and stocked with small fish. A few "wild" catfish are caught in rivers, lakes and ponds.

SELECTION AND HANDLING: The flesh of fresh catfish should be white or off-white and have no fish odor. Avoid any with red, brown, gray or yellow coloring. Look for fresh or frozen catfish sold whole or cut into fillets or steaks. Whole fish average 1 to 1½ pounds (454 to 680g) each, and fillets average 5 to 15 ounces (142 to 426g) each.

FLAVOR: Farm-raised catfish taste mild with a slight sweetness due to their controlled diet of grains, vitamins and minerals. Wild catfish may taste slightly "muddy," but they are rarely sold commercially.

FLESH: Firm texture with a slight flakiness.

PREPARATION: Traditionally coated with cornmeal and fried, catfish also taste great grilled, broiled or baked.

Prep Time: 10 minutes
Cook Time: 5 minutes

½ tsp. (2.5ml) chili powder
¼ tsp. (1ml) salt
1 lb. (454g) fresh or thawed catfish fillets, about ½ inch (1.3cm) thick
½ cup (118ml) chopped green bell pepper
¼ cup (59ml) finely chopped onion
¼ tsp. (1ml) chili powder
1 tbsp. (15ml) vegetable oil
1 (8-oz./227ml) can whole kernel corn, drained

1 Preheat oven to 450°F/232°C. Lightly coat a baking dish with nonstick cooking spray.

2 In a small bowl combine ½ teaspoon (2.4 millilitres) of the chili powder and salt. Rinse fish; pat dry with paper towels. Cut catfish into 4 serving-size pieces. Sprinkle fillets with chili powder mixture. Place in the shallow baking dish. Tuck under any thin edges of fish. Bake, uncovered, for 5 to 6 minutes or until fish flakes with a fork (145°F/63°C).

3 Meanwhile, in a medium skillet cook pepper, onion and ¼ teaspoon (1 millilitre) chili powder in hot oil for 2 minutes. Stir in corn. Cook, stirring occasionally, until heated through.

4 Serve corn relish over catfish.

Makes 4 servings

U.S. Per Serving: 219 calories, 18g carbohydrate, 20g protein, 9g fat, 2g fiber, 62mg cholesterol, 273mg sodium, 0g Omega-3
Canada Per Serving: 915.46 kJ, 19.82g protein, 9g fat, 17.66g carbohydrate, 1.82g dietary fibre, 273.27mg sodium, 168.60mg potassium, 0.01g Omega-3

catfish with mustard sauce

Prep Time: 5 minutes
Cook Time: 5 minutes

4 (8-oz./227g) fresh or thawed catfish fillets, about ¹/₂ inch (1.3cm) thick
2 to 3 tbsp. (30 to 44ml) Dijon-style mustard
⅓ cup (79ml) chopped pecans, toasted
2 tbsp. (30ml) chopped fresh chives
4 lemon wedges

1 Preheat the broiler. Lightly coat the rack of a broiler pan with nonstick cooking spray; set aside.

2 Rinse fish; pat dry with paper towels. Place fillets on the broiler pan rack. Tuck under any thin edges of fish. Season with salt and pepper. Spread mustard on top of fillets.

3 Broil 4 to 5 inches (10 to 13 centimetres) from the heat for 5 to 6 minutes or until fish flakes with a fork (145°F/63°C).

4 Place each fillet on a plate with a lemon wedge. Sprinkle with pecans and chives.

Makes 4 servings

U.S. Per Serving: 343 calories, 12g carbohydrate, 37g protein, 18g fat, 1g fiber, 124mg cholesterol, 45mg sodium, 0g Omega-3
Canada Per Serving: 1433.11 kJ, 37.43g protein, 17.52g fat, 11.84g carbohydrate, 1.12g dietary fibre, 44.64mg sodium, 58.42mg potassium, 0.10g Omega-3

catfish

Prep Time: 5 minutes
Cook Time: 5 minutes

1½ lb. (680g) fresh or thawed catfish fillets, about ½ inch (1.3cm) thick
1 tbsp. (15ml) vegetable oil
2 tbsp. (30ml) lemon pepper seasoning

1   Preheat the boiler. Lightly coat the rack of a broiler pan with nonstick cooking spray.

2   Rinse fish; pat dry with paper towels. Cut fillets into 6 serving-size pieces. Place fillets on the broiler pan rack. Tuck under any thin edges of fish.

3   Lightly brush fillets with oil. Sprinkle with lemon pepper seasoning. Broil 4 to 5 inches (10 to 13 centimetres) from the heat for 5 to 6 minutes or until fish flakes with a fork (145°F/63°C).

Makes 6 servings

U.S. Per Serving: 152 calories, 5g carbohydrate, 18g protein, 7g fat, 0g fiber, 62mg cholesterol, 321mg sodium, 0g Omega-3
Canada Per Serving: 637.36 kJ, 18g protein, 7.17g fat, 4.80g carbohydrate, 0g dietary fibre, 321mg sodium, 0mg potassium, 0g Omega-3

catfish fillets with cornbread stuffing

Prep time: 10 minutes
Cook time: 9 minutes
Standing time: 5 minutes

1 to 1¼ lb. (454g to 567g) fresh or thawed catfish fillets, about ½ inch (1.3cm) thick
Paprika (optional)
2 tbsp. (30ml) butter or margarine
1 medium cooking apple, cored and chopped
½ cup (118ml) sliced celery
1½ cups (355ml) water
1 (6-oz./170g) pkg. seasoned cornbread stuffing mix
Apple wedges (optional)

1   Rinse fish; pat dry with paper towels. Season catfish with salt, pepper and paprika, if desired. In a large nonstick skillet cook catfish in hot butter for 3 minutes; add apple and celery. Cook 3 to 4 minutes more or until fish flakes with a fork (145°F/63°C).

2   Remove catfish; keep warm. Add water to the same skillet; bring to a boil. Stir in dry stuffing mix and seasoning packet, if present. Cover and let stand 5 minutes.

3   Serve stuffing with catfish. Garnish with apple wedges, if desired.

Makes 4 servings

U.S. Per Serving: 398 calories, 38g carbohydrate, 22g protein, 17g fat, 7g fiber, 68mg cholesterol, 619mg sodium, 0g Omega-3
Canada Per Serving: 1647.94 kJ, 22.06g protein, 16.54g fat, 38.43g carbohydrate, 7.27g dietary fibre, 618.75mg sodium, 508.54mg potassium, 0.43g Omega-3

clams

Hardshell clams describes many varieties such as quahog, chowder clams, littleneck, top neck, count neck, cherry stone, hard clams, butter clams, cockle, pismo clams and baby clams.

SOURCE: They are found in both the shallow and deep cool waters of the Atlantic and Pacific oceans. Many farm-raised clams come from the southern United States.

SELECTION & HANDLING: Clams in the shell must be alive until ready to eat or cook. Look for shells that are tightly closed or ones that close when tapped. Smaller clams are more tender than larger ones. Refrigerate live clams in a bowl or mesh bag, covered with wet paper towels. Never store them in airtight containers or cover them with plastic wrap. Keep them cold, but not on ice.

FLAVOR: Moderate and slightly salty.

FLESH: Somewhat chewy.

PREPARATION: Scrub the outside of the shells with a stiff brush and cold water before cooking. Clams can be steamed, baked, or eaten raw by healthy individuals.

NOTE: Elderly people, pregnant women, children and people with compromised immune systems (including those with liver disease, AIDS, diabetes, cancer, gastrointestinal disorders, cirrhosis, lymphoma, inflammatory bowel disease, steroid dependency, or kidney disease) should NEVER eat raw shellfish.

Prep Time: 20 minutes
Cook Time: 35 minutes

12 clams
4 chicken drumsticks or thighs
4 ears fresh corn, husked and cleaned
12 oz. (340g) cooked smoked reduced-fat sausage link, cut into 4 pieces
⅓ cup (79ml) butter or margarine
2 tbsp. (30ml) chopped fresh chives or basil

1 Lightly coat the grill rack with nonstick cooking spray. Preheat the grill to medium.

2 Scrub clams under cold water. Drain. Set aside.

3 Remove skin from chicken, if desired. Rinse chicken; pat dry with paper towels. Season chicken with salt and pepper.

4 Grill chicken for 35 to 45 minutes or until tender and no longer pink (170°F/77°C), turning occasionally. Place corn on the grill 10 minutes after starting chicken, cooking 25 to 30 minutes or until tender, turning occasionally. Add sausage pieces the last 10 minutes of cooking, turning sausage once. Add clams the last 5 minutes of cooking. Carefully watch clams as they cook; remove from grill as they open. Discard any clams that do not open.

5 Meanwhile, melt the butter and stir in chives.

6 Serve butter for brushing on corn and dipping clams.

Makes 4 servings

U.S. Per Serving: 524 calories, 21g carbohydrate, 36g protein, 37g fat, 2g fiber, 165mg cholesterol, 667mg sodium, 0g Omega-3

Canada Per Serving: 2192.07 kJ, 36.27g protein, 37.12g fat, 20.80g carbohydrate, 2.47g dietary fibre, 667.47mg sodium, 524.15mg potassium, 0.12g Omega-3

clams in white wine broth

Prep Time: 20 minutes
Cook Time: 13 minutes

72 small clams
1 cup (237ml) dry white wine
1 cup (237ml) chopped onion
1 tbsp. (15ml) chopped fresh parsley
1 tbsp. (15ml) butter or margarine
1 tsp. (5ml) dried thyme, crushed
1 bay leaf
Dash freshly ground black pepper
Sliced French bread

1 Scrub clams under cold water. Drain.

2 In a large kettle combine wine, onion, parsley, butter, thyme, bay leaf and pepper. Add clams. Bring to a boil; reduce heat. Cover and simmer for 10 to 15 minutes or until clams open. Simmer 3 minutes more. Discard any clams that do not open.

3 Place clams in shallow bowls. Keep warm. Strain liquid through cheesecloth. Ladle hot liquid over clams. Serve with French bread.

Makes 6 servings

U.S. Per Serving: 138 calories, 6g carbohydrate, 14g protein, 3g fat, 1g fiber, 42mg cholesterol, 64mg sodium, 0g Omega-3

Canada Per Serving: 577.38 kJ, 14.17g protein, 3.10g fat, 5.66g carbohydrate, 0.60g dietary fibre, 63.69mg sodium, 419.01mg potassium, 0.16g Omega-3

clams

Prep Time: 15 minutes
Cook Time: 15 minutes

  2 medium potatoes, peeled and cut into ½-inch (1.3cm) cubes
  1 (8-oz./227g) bottle clam juice
  1 cup (237ml) thinly sliced celery
  ½ cup (118ml) chopped onion
  ½ cup (118ml) chopped carrot
  ½ tsp. (2.5ml) dried thyme, crushed
  1 pint (473ml) fresh shucked clams or 2 (6½-oz./184g) cans minced clams
  1 (14½-oz./411g) can stewed tomatoes, chopped

1 In a 3-quart (2.85-litre) saucepan combine potatoes, clam juice, celery, onion, carrot and thyme. Bring to a boil; reduce heat. Cover and simmer for 10 minutes or until potatoes are tender, stirring occasionally.

2 Stir in clams and undrained tomatoes. Bring to a boil; reduce heat. Cover and simmer for 5 minutes.

Makes 4 servings

U.S. Per Serving: 642 calories, 135g carbohydrate, 37g protein, 2g fat, 17g fiber, 54mg cholesterol, 3168mg sodium, 0g Omega-3
Canada Per Serving: 2686.90 kJ, 37.34g protein, 1.66g fat, 135.44g carbohydrate, 17.43g dietary fibre, 3167.87mg sodium, 1138.48mg potassium, 0.24g Omega-3

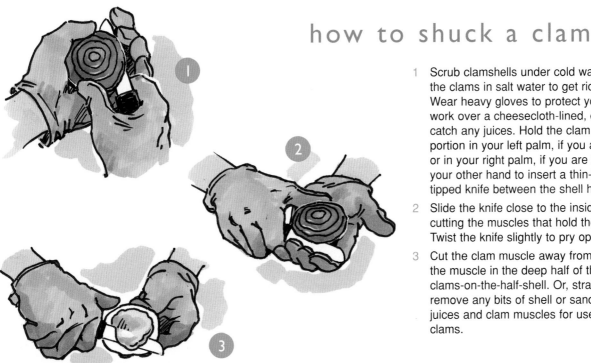

how to shuck a clam

1 Scrub clamshells under cold water, then soak the clams in salt water to get rid of any sand. Wear heavy gloves to protect your hands and work over a cheesecloth-lined, clean bowl to catch any juices. Hold the clam with the hinged portion in your left palm, if you are right-handed, or in your right palm, if you are left handed. Use your other hand to insert a thin-bladed, blunt-tipped knife between the shell halves.

2 Slide the knife close to the inside of the shells, cutting the muscles that hold the shell together. Twist the knife slightly to pry open the shells.

3 Cut the clam muscle away from the shell. Place the muscle in the deep half of the shell for clams-on-the-half-shell. Or, strain the juices to remove any bits of shell or sand. Combine the juices and clam muscles for use as shucked clams.

cod

Cod is one of the most versatile and popular fish. It is sold fresh, frozen, salted, smoked, pickled and as breaded fish sticks. It also holds an important place in history, as it can be preserved by smoking, salting and drying and served as an ideal source of protein prior to refrigeration.

SOURCE: Traditional sources of cod include the northern Atlantic coastal regions of Canada and the United States. More recently, the frigid waters of the Gulf of Alaska and the Bering Sea have become major suppliers.

SELECTION & HANDLING: Cod can range from 3 to 245 pounds (1.4 to 111kg). The term scrod more accurately refers to smaller cod, those weighing less than 2½ pounds (1.1kg). Avoid fish fillets with separating, as this indicates age. Be sure to cook cod to 145°F/63°C before eating because parasites are a potential hazard.

FLAVOR: Very mild.

FLESH: Firm with very large flakes.

PREPARATION: Cod may be prepared by any cooking method and is especially suited to baking, broiling, steaming and poaching.

Prep Time: 15 minutes
Cook Time: 8 minutes

2 (6-oz./170g) fresh or thawed cod fillets, about ½ inch (1.3cm) thick
¼ cup (59ml) flour
2 tbsp. (30ml) butter or margarine
1 cup (237ml) peeled and sliced cucumber
1 clove garlic, minced
1 tsp. (5ml) chopped fresh dill weed
1 tbsp. (15ml) lemon juice

1   Rinse fish; pat dry with paper towels. Coat fish with flour. Season with salt and pepper.

2   In a large skillet heat butter. Add fish. Cook over medium heat for 5 to 6 minutes or until fish flakes with a fork (145°F/63°C), turning once. Transfer to a warm platter.

3   Add cucumber, garlic and dill to skillet. Cook for 2 minutes. Add lemon juice. Cook 1 minute more. Spoon over cod.

Makes 2 servings

U.S. Per Serving: 308 calories, 15g carbohydrate, 32g protein, 14g fat, 1g fiber, 30mg cholesterol, 204mg sodium, 0g Omega-3
Canada Per Serving: 1289.40 kJ, 32.08g protein, 13.76g fat, 14.57g carbohydrate, 0.90g dietary fibre, 204.39mg sodium, 120.93mg potassium, 0.03g Omega-3

cod with tomato pesto

Prep Time: 5 minutes
Cook Time: 10 minutes

1¼ lb. (567g) fresh or thawed cod fillets, about 1 inch (2.5cm) thick
2 plum tomatoes, chopped
¼ cup (59ml) chopped fresh Italian parsley
¼ cup (59ml) grated Parmesan cheese
2 tbsp. (30ml) chopped fresh basil or ½ tsp. (2.5ml) dried basil, crushed
1 clove garlic, minced

1   Preheat the broiler. Lightly coat the rack of a broiler pan with nonstick cooking spray; set aside.

2   Rinse fish; pat dry with paper towels. Cut fish into 4 serving-size pieces. Place on the broiler pan rack. Tuck under any thin pieces of fish. Season with salt and pepper.

3   Broil 4 to 5 inches (10 to 13 centimetres) from the heat for 9 to 10 minutes or until almost done, turning once.

4   Meanwhile, for tomato pesto stir together tomatoes, parsley, Parmesan cheese, basil and garlic.

5   Top fish with tomato pesto. Broil 1 to 2 minutes more or until fish flakes with a fork (145°F/63°C) and pesto is warm.

Makes 4 servings

U.S. Per Serving: 156 calories, 2g carbohydrate, 29g protein, 3g fat, 0g fiber, 64mg cholesterol, 194mg sodium, 0g Omega-3
Canada Per Serving: 651.10 kJ, 28.72g protein, 3.34g fat, 1.98g carbohydrate, 0.41g dietary fibre, 194.14mg sodium, 681.69mg potassium, 0.26g Omega-3

cod

Prep Time: 10 minutes
Cook Time: 10 minutes

4 (6-oz./170g) fresh or thawed cod fillets, about 1 inch (2.5cm) thick
2 shallots, chopped
1 tbsp. (15ml) butter or margarine
4 cups (.95l) hot milk
1 tsp. (5ml) chopped fresh parsley
Lemon wedges

1 Rinse fish; pat dry with paper towels.

2 In a large skillet cook shallots in butter until tender. Carefully stir in milk and parsley. Bring to a boil.

3 Gently add cod to milk mixture. Return to a boil; reduce heat. Cover and simmer for 10 to 11 minutes or until fish flakes with a fork (145°F/63°C).

4 Transfer cod to a warm serving platter. Serve with lemon wedges.

Makes 4 servings

U.S. Per Serving: 352 calories, 15g carbohydrate, 50g protein, 9g fat, 0g fiber, 126mg cholesterol, 249mg sodium, 1g Omega-3
Canada Per Serving: 1470.35 kJ, 49.78g protein, 9.26g fat, 15.09g carbohydrate, 0.01g dietary fibre, 249.32mg sodium, 1398.32mg potassium, 0.50g Omega-3

cod á la French country

Prep Time: 10 minutes
Cook Time: 5 minutes

4 (6-oz./170g) fresh or thawed cod fillets, about ½ inch (1.3cm) thick
4 tsp. (20ml) olive oil
4 plum tomatoes, chopped
4 ripe olives, sliced
Dash dried thyme, crushed
4 tsp. (20ml) olive oil
1 tsp. (5ml) dried basil, crushed

1 Rinse fish; pat dry with paper towels. Season fillets with salt and pepper.

2 In a large skillet heat 4 teaspoons (20 millilitres) of the oil. Add cod fillets. Cook over medium-high heat for 1 minute, turning once.

3 Sprinkle tomatoes, olives and thyme over cod. Reduce heat. Cover and cook for 2 minutes.

4 Drizzle with remaining 4 teaspoons (20 millilitres) olive oil and sprinkle with basil. Cook, covered, for 2 to 3 minutes more or until fish flakes with a fork (145°F/63°C).

Makes 4 servings

U.S. Per Serving: 247 calories, 4g carbohydrate, 31g protein, 13g fat, 1g fiber, 0mg cholesterol, 318mg sodium, 0g Omega-3
Canada Per Serving: 1034.61 kJ, 30.63g protein, 13.04g fat, 4g carbohydrate, 0.79g dietary fibre, 318.19mg sodium, 144.71mg potassium, 0g Omega-3

crab

Crab refers to nearly 4,000 varieties of crustaceans. Blue crabs are named for their blue claws and blue-green shells. Pacific Dungeness crabs range from 1 to 4 pounds (454g to 1.82kg), while king crabs may be 8 feet (2.4m) across and weigh up to 15 pounds (6.8kg). Snow crabs average 5 pounds (2.27kg) and measure 2 feet (61cm) from tip to tip.

SOURCE: The Pacific Ocean yields the Dungeness crabs. The north Pacific provides king crabs and snow crabs. Snow crabs are also found on Canada's eastern shores. Blue crabs come from the coastlines of the Atlantic Ocean and the Gulf of Mexico.

SELECTION & HANDLING: Crabs are found in many forms. They are sold whole, both live and cooked. Fresh and frozen crab meat is sold as clusters, legs or picked meat. Soft-shell crabs are whole blue crabs removed from the water immediately after molting. Refrigerate live crabs in moist packaging for up to 24 hours. Do not place in airtight containers, water or salted water. Make sure live crabs are still moving before cooking. Unopened, pasteurized crab meat will last up to 2 months in the refrigerator, but should be used within 2 days of opening. Clusters, legs or picked meat that is not pasteurized should be used within a day or two of purchase.

FLAVOR: Sweet.

FLESH: Firm and tender. Body meat is white and flakes easily. Claw meat has brownish tinges.

PREPARATION: Prepare live crabs by steaming or simmering. Any commercial "crab boil" may be added for seasoning. Cooked legs or clusters may be heated by broiling, steaming or simmering. Use picked meat in salads, crab cakes and stuffings.

Prep Time: 20 minutes
Cook Time: 20 minutes

8 lb. (3.64kg) hard-shell blue crabs
3 cups (710ml) white vinegar
3 cups (710ml) beer
2 tbsp. (30ml) seafood seasoning
2 tbsp. (30ml) salt

1 Grasp live crabs from behind, firmly holding back two legs on each side.
   Rinse under cold water. Set aside.

2 In a very large steamer pot combine vinegar and beer. Bring to a boil.
   Add crabs to steaming rack, sprinkling some seafood seasoning and salt between each layer of crab.

3 Return to a boil; reduce heat. Cover and simmer for 15 to 25 minutes or until crab shells turn bright orange and crab
   meat is opaque.

Makes 8 servings

U.S. Per Serving: 442 calories, 8g carbohydrate, 83g protein, 5g fat, 0g fiber, 354mg cholesterol, 3560mg sodium, 1g Omega-3
Canada Per Serving: 1851.43 kJ, 82.56g protein, 5.27g fat, 7.98g carbohydrate, 0.18g dietary fibre, 3559.51mg sodium, 1514.98mg potassium, 1.46g Omega-3

crabcakes with herb sauce

Prep Time: 20 minutes
Cook Time: 12 minutes

¼ cup (59ml) mayonnaise
1 tbsp. (15ml) chopped fresh dill weed
2 tsp. (10ml) chopped fresh chives
2 tsp. (10ml) chopped fresh parsley
2 tsp. (10ml) lemon juice
1 tsp. (5ml) Dijon-style mustard
Dash ground red pepper
¾ lb. (341ml) fresh or thawed
   crab meat

1¼ cups (296ml) fresh bread
   crumbs (about 1½ slices)
¼ cup (59ml) mayonnaise
3 tbsp. (33ml) finely chopped onion
1 tsp. (5ml) dry mustard
¾ tsp. (4ml) salt
¼ tsp. (1ml) bottled
   hot pepper sauce
Lemon wedges

1 For sauce stir together ¼ cup (59 millilitres) of the mayonnaise, dill weed,
   chives, parsley, lemon juice, mustard and red pepper. Cover and refrigerate
   until serving time.

2 Lightly coat a grill rack or grill basket with nonstick cooking spray. Preheat
   the grill to medium.

3 In a large mixing bowl toss together crab meat, crumbs, remaining ¼ cup
   (59 millilitres) mayonnaise, onion, mustard, salt and hot pepper sauce.
   Shape into four ½-inch (1.3-centimetre) thick patties.

4 Place patties on the grill rack or in the grill basket. Grill for 12 to 18 minutes
   or until light brown, turning once.

5 Serve crab cakes with herb sauce and lemon wedges.

Makes 4 servings

U.S. Per Serving: 426 calories, 25g carbohydrate, 23g protein, 25g fat, 1g fiber,
70mg cholesterol, 1159mg sodium, 0g Omega-3
Canada Per Serving: 1781.65 kJ, 23.38g protein, 25.14g fat, 25.15g carbohydrate,
1.48g dietary fibre, 1159.34mg sodium, 23.25mg potassium, 0g Omega-3

crab

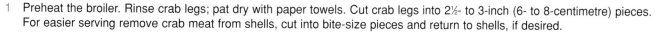

Prep Time: 25 minutes
Cook Time: 3 minutes

12 oz. (340g) thawed king crab legs, split
¼ cup (59ml) butter or margarine, melted
1 tbsp. (15ml) lemon juice
1 tbsp. (5ml) chopped fresh parsley
2 tsp. (10ml) grated onion
1 clove garlic, minced
¼ tsp. (1ml) dried tarragon, crushed
Dash bottled hot pepper sauce

1 Preheat the broiler. Rinse crab legs; pat dry with paper towels. Cut crab legs into 2½- to 3-inch (6- to 8-centimetre) pieces. For easier serving remove crab meat from shells, cut into bite-size pieces and return to shells, if desired.

2 In a small bowl stir together butter, lemon juice, parsley, onion, garlic, tarragon and hot pepper sauce. Brush over crab.

3 Place crab legs, shell-side down, on the broiler pan rack. Broil 4 to 5 inches (10 to 13 centimetres) from the heat for 3 to 4 minutes or until heated through, brushing occasionally with butter mixture.

Makes 2 servings

U.S. Per Serving: 359 calories, 2g carbohydrate, 31g protein, 25g fat, 0g fiber, 131mg cholesterol, 1428mg sodium, 0g Omega-3
Canada Per Serving: 1500.87 kJ, 31.31g protein, 25.05g fat, 1.56g carbohydrate, 0.18g dietary fibre, 1428.32mg sodium, 378.03mg potassium, 0g Omega-3

king crab royale

snow crab and tarragon pasta

Prep Time: 15 minutes
Cook Time: 15 minutes

1 lb. (454g) dried penne or bowtie pasta
2 shallots, chopped
2 tbsp. (30ml) olive oil
12 oz. (340g) thawed snow crab meat (about 1½ lb./680g snow crab legs)
⅓ cup (79ml) lemon juice
1 tsp. (5ml) chopped fresh tarragon

1 Cook pasta according to package directions. Drain; keep warm.

2 Meanwhile, in a large skillet cook shallots in hot olive oil until tender. Stir in crab meat. Cook and stir about 3 minutes or until heated through. Stir in lemon juice and tarragon. Season with salt and pepper.

3 Pour crab mixture over pasta; toss to mix.

Makes 4 servings

U.S. Per Serving: 520 calories, 73g carbohydrate, 32g protein, 10g fat, 12g fiber, 0mg cholesterol, 293mg sodium, 0g Omega-3
Canada Per Serving: 2174.89 kJ, 31.58g protein, 10.02g fat, 73.16g carbohydrate, 12.08g dietary fibre, 292.60mg sodium, 95.21mg potassium, 0g Omega-3

crab

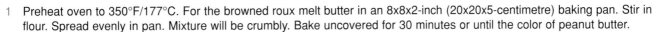

Prep Time: 5 minutes
Cook Time: 45 minutes

crab étouffée

2 tbsp. (30ml) butter
⅓ cup (79ml) flour
1 to 1½ lb. (454 to 680g) king crab legs or snow crab legs, thawed
1 cup (237ml) each chopped onion, celery and red or green bell pepper
2 cloves garlic, chopped
Hot pepper sauce
½ cup (118ml) sliced green onions
2 cups (473ml) hot cooked rice (⅔ cup/158ml uncooked)

1   Preheat oven to 350°F/177°C. For the browned roux melt butter in an 8x8x2-inch (20x20x5-centimetre) baking pan. Stir in flour. Spread evenly in pan. Mixture will be crumbly. Bake uncovered for 30 minutes or until the color of peanut butter.

2   Meanwhile, use kitchen scissors to cut shell from crab legs or use a crab cracker. Remove meat. Pick out cartilage and break into chunks.

3   Transfer roux to a 3-quart (2.85-litre) saucepan. Add vegetables; cook, covered, over low heat stirring occasionally for 10 minutes or until vegetables are very tender. Stir in 2 cups (473 millilitres) water and pepper sauce to taste. Cook and stir until thickened and bubbly. Stir in crab meat and green onions. Heat through. Season with salt and pepper. Serve over hot cooked rice. Pass additional hot sauce and garnish with parsley, if desired.

Makes 4 servings

U.S. Per Serving: 322 calories, 38g carbohydrate, 25g protein, 7g fat, 3g fiber, 63mg cholesterol, 980mg sodium, 0g Omega-3
Canada Per Serving: 1348.59 kJ, 25.19g protein, 7.21g fat, 38.06g carbohydrate, 2.90g dietary fibre, 980.47mg sodium, 519.38mg potassium, 0.02g Omega-3

surimi crab salad

Prep Time: 10 minutes

12 oz. (340g) imitation crab meat (surimi), flaked
1 small avocado, halved, seeded, peeled and chopped
¾ cup (178ml) shredded carrots
¾ cup (178ml) thinly sliced celery
2 tbsp. (30ml) mayonnaise
2 tbsp. (30ml) plain yogurt
2 tbsp. (30ml) prepared creamy horseradish
1 tsp. (5ml) lemon juice
4 large romaine lettuce leaves

1   In a medium bowl toss together crab, avocado, carrots and celery.

2   In a small bowl stir together mayonnaise, yogurt, horseradish and lemon juice. Add to crab mixture. Toss gently.

3   Serve on lettuce leaves.

Makes 4 servings

U.S. Per Serving: 245 calories, 17g carbohydrate, 12g protein, 15g fat, 4g fiber, 20mg cholesterol, 830mg sodium, 1g Omega-3
Canada Per Serving: 1024.27 kJ, 12.13g protein, 14.66g fat, 16.95g carbohydrate, 3.76g dietary fibre, 830.46mg sodium, 546.53mg potassium, 0.59g Omega-3

crab

Prep Time: 10 minutes
Cook Time: 5 minutes

1½ cups (355ml) chopped papaya or mango
3 tbsp. (44ml) chopped jalapeño pepper
1 tbsp. (15ml) thawed orange juice concentrate
8 (8-inch/20cm) flour tortillas
12 oz. (340g) imitation crab meat (surimi), flaked
1½ cups (355ml) shredded Havarti cheese (6 oz./170g)
¼ cup (59ml) sliced green onions

1 Spray grill rack with nonstick cooking spray. Preheat grill to medium.

2 In a small bowl stir together papaya or mango, jalapeño pepper and orange juice concentrate. Set aside.

3 Place 4 flour tortillas on the grill rack. Quickly sprinkle with imitation crab meat, cheese and green onions. Top with remaining tortillas, pressing down slightly on each. Grill for 5 to 7 minutes or until lightly toasted, turning once. Cut each into 6 wedges. Serve with papaya mixture.

Makes 24 appetizer servings

Recipe Note:
Always wear plastic gloves or slip plastic bags over hands when working with hot peppers to avoid possible burning or irritation of your skin.

U.S. Per Serving: 69 calories, 7g carbohydrate, 4g protein, 3g fat, 2g fiber, 12mg cholesterol, 215mg sodium, 0g Omega-3
Canada Per Serving: 287.43 kJ, 3.95g protein, 2.95g fat, 6.83g carbohydrate, 2.20g dietary fibre, 214.58mg sodium, 40.87mg potassium, 0.09g Omega-3

how to crack a cooked hard-shell crab

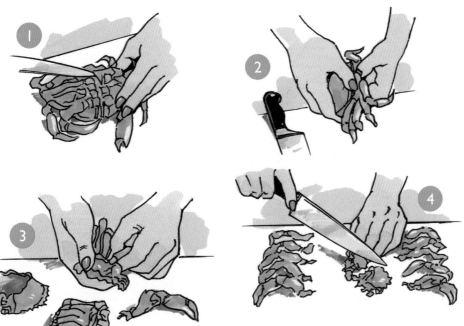

1 Turn the crab on its back. Using the tip of a knife, pry up the tail flap or apron, then use your fingers to twist it off. Discard the tail flap.

2 Hold the crab with the top shell in one hand and grasp the bottom shell with the other. Pull the top shell away from the body and discard. Remove and discard the internal organs, the mouth, and appendages from the front of the crab. Rinse the crab. Using a small knife remove the spongy gills from both sides of the top of the crab.

3 Twist legs and claws off the body. Use a nutcracker or clean pliers to crack each joint. Pick out the meat.

4 Cut the crab body into quarters. Remove the remaining meat with a pick or small fork.

flounder

Flounder are part of a large species of flatfish with bodies compressed laterally into flat oval shapes. They are valued for their fine texture and delicate flavor. Some members of the flounder family include dab and plaice. Many fish marketed in North America as fillet of sole are actually flounders.

SOURCE: Gray sole flounder and lemon sole flounder are found in the North Atlantic. Rock sole flounder is found along the Pacific coast. Dab flounder and yellowtail flounder are found along both northern coasts of North America.

SELECTION & HANDLING: Depending on the species, the size of the flounder varies from 4 ounces to 20 pounds (113g to 9kg). They are sold whole, dressed or as fillets.

FLAVOR: Delicate.

FLESH: Firm and white with a fine texture.

PREPARATION: Flounder may be cooked by almost any method. They may be combined with a variety of flavors without losing their identity. Whole flounder are often stuffed.

Prep Time: 5 minutes
Cook Time: 10 minutes

4 (5-oz./142g) flounder fillets, about ¾ inch (1.9cm) thick
1 (8-oz./227g) pkg. cream cheese, softened
¼ cup (59ml) oil-packed dried tomatoes, drained and cut up
1 tsp. (5ml) dried basil, crushed
3 tbsp. (44ml) chopped fresh parsley
2 tbsp. (30ml) lemon juice

1 Preheat oven to 450ºF/232°C. Lightly coat a baking dish with nonstick cooking spray.

2 Place fillets in the baking dish. Tuck under any thin edges of fish. In a small bowl stir together cream cheese, tomatoes and basil.

3 Top fillets with cream cheese mixture. Sprinkle with parsley and lemon juice. Bake for 10 to 15 minutes or until fish flakes with a fork (145°F/63°C). Spoon pan juices over fish.

Makes 4 servings

U.S. Per Serving: 354 calories, 4g carbohydrate, 32g protein, 23g fat, 1g fiber, 118mg cholesterol, 320mg sodium, 0g Omega-3
Canada Per Serving: 1482.48 kJ, 32.48g protein, 23.32g fat, 4.22g carbohydrate, 0.57g dietary fibre, 319.92mg sodium, 132.84mg potassium, 0g Omega-3

lemon & parsley flounder

Prep Time: 10 minutes
Cook Time: 7 minutes

4 (5-oz./142g) fresh or thawed flounder fillets, about ¾ inch (1.9cm) thick
⅓ cup (79ml) flour
2 tbsp. (30ml) vegetable oil
1 tbsp. (15ml) butter or margarine
1 tbsp. (15ml) lemon juice
1 tbsp. (15ml) chopped fresh parsley

1 Rinse fish; pat dry with paper towels. In a shallow dish stir together flour and salt and pepper to taste. Coat fish with flour mixture.

2 In a large skillet heat oil and butter. Add fish. Cook over medium-high heat for 7 to 8 minutes or until fish flakes with a fork (145°F/63°C), turning once.

3 Transfer fish to a warm platter. Pour pan juice over fish. Sprinkle with lemon juice and parsley.

Makes 4 servings

U.S. Per Serving: 256 calories, 8g carbohydrate, 28g protein, 12g fat, 0g fiber, 76mg cholesterol, 116mg sodium, 0g Omega-3
Canada Per Serving: 1069.78 kJ, 27.82g protein, 11.59g fat, 8.38g carbohydrate, 0.34g dietary fibre, 115.53mg sodium, 533.33mg potassium, 0.30g Omega-3

grouper

Grouper are members of the large and prolific sea bass family. They are also commonly called sand perch, rock cod, coney and jewfish. The most commonly marketed species include the black and red groupers.

SOURCE: Grouper come from the Gulf of Mexico, north and south Atlantic Ocean, Pacific Ocean and the Caribbean.

SELECTION & HANDLING: While grouper may weigh 100 pounds (45.4kg) or more, most market fish range from 5 to 10 pounds (2.3 to 4.5kg). Avoid fish larger than 10 pounds (4.5kg). Grouper have no intramuscular bones, which makes them ideal for filleting.

FLAVOR: Mild and sweet.

FLESH: Firm with very large flakes.

PREPARATION: Grouper skin is tough and bitter and should be removed before cooking. The meat is firm enough to cut into cubes for kabobs or to use in soups or chowders. The large flakes of cooked grouper make it great for salads. Grouper can be cut into thick slices, then battered and deep-fried. It is excellent baked, poached, steamed, broiled or grilled.

Prep Time: 10 minutes
Cook Time: 7 minutes

¼ cup (59ml) butter or margarine
2 tsp. (10ml) soy sauce
1 tsp. (5ml) lemon juice or lime juice
½ tsp. (2.5ml) Worcestershire sauce
⅛ tsp. (.62ml) pepper
2 lb. (907g) fresh or thawed grouper fillets, about ¾ inch (1.9cm) thick

1 Lightly coat a grill basket with nonstick cooking spray; set aside. Preheat the grill to medium.

2 In a small saucepan combine butter, soy sauce, lemon juice, Worcestershire sauce and pepper. Cook and stir over medium heat until butter is melted and ingredients are combined. Set aside.

3 Rinse fish; pat dry with paper towels. Cut fish into 6 serving-size pieces. Place fish in the grill basket. Tuck under any thin edges of fish. Grill for 7 to 9 minutes or until fish flakes with a fork (145°F/63°C), turning once and brushing frequently with butter mixture.

Makes 6 servings

U.S. Per Serving: 211 calories, 0g carbohydrate, 29g protein, 10g fat, 0g fiber, 76mg cholesterol, 196mg sodium, 0g Omega-3
Canada Per Serving: 881.67 kJ, 29.36g protein, 9.54g fat, 0.34g carbohydrate, 0.02g dietary fibre, 195.59mg sodium, 735.98mg potassium, 0.39g Omega-3

blackened grouper

Prep Time: 15 minutes
Cook Time: 7 minutes

1½ lb. (680g) fresh or thawed grouper fillets, about ¾ inch (1.9cm) thick
1 tbsp. (15ml) paprika
1 tsp. (5ml) dried thyme, crushed
1 tsp. (5ml) ground red pepper
1 tsp. (5ml) freshly ground black pepper
¼ tsp. (1ml) ground allspice
1 tbsp. (15ml) butter or margarine, melted
1 tsp. (5ml) vegetable oil

1 Lightly coat a grill rack or the rack of a broiler pan with nonstick cooking spray. Preheat the broiler or grill to medium.

2 In a shallow dish combine paprika, thyme, red pepper, black pepper and allspice. In a small dish stir together butter and oil.

3 Rinse fish; pat dry with paper towels. Cut into 4 serving-size pieces. Brush fish with butter mixture. Dip grouper into spice mix, turning to coat both sides. Place on the broiler pan rack or grill rack. Tuck under any thin edges of fish.

4 Broil fish 4 to 5 inches (10 to 13 centimetres) from the heat for 7 to 9 minutes or until fish flakes with a fork (145°F/63°C), turning once. Or, grill fish for 7 to 9 minutes or until fish flakes with a fork (145°F/63°C), turning once.

Makes 4 servings

U.S. Per Serving: 59.45 calories, 2g carbohydrate, 2g protein, 5g fat, 1g fiber, 11mg cholesterol, 7mg sodium, 0g Omega-3
Canada Per Serving: 248.72 kJ, 2.35g protein, 4.54g fat, 1.54g carbohydrate, 0.50g dietary fibre, 6.61mg sodium, 92.51mg potassium, 0.04g Omega-3

haddock

A member of the cod family, haddock are distinguished from their cousins by a dark lateral line along their sides and a dark spot on their shoulders known, oddly, as both "the devil's thumbprint" and "St. Peter's mark." Haddock are smaller than cod.

SOURCE: Haddock are harvested year-round in the North Atlantic from Newfoundland south to New England and also in the waters off northern Europe.

SELECTION & HANDLING: In North America whole haddock are commonly sold fresh. Fresh or frozen fillets and steaks are always sold skin-on to retain their identity.

FLAVOR: Delicate and mild.

FLESH: White, somewhat finer than cod. Firm texture.

PREPARATION: Haddock may be prepared in a variety of ways, including baking, poaching, sautéing and grilling. Because of its mild flavor, haddock should be seasoned lightly.

haddock dilly

Prep Time: 10 minutes
Chill Time: 1 hour
Cook Time: 10 minutes

½ cup (118ml) plain yogurt
½ cup (118ml) peeled, chopped cucumber
3 tbsp. (44ml) mayonnaise
1 tbsp. (15ml) chopped fresh dill weed
1½ lb. (690g) fresh or thawed haddock fillets, about 1 inch (2.5cm) thick
3 cups water
½ cup (118ml) dry white wine

1   In a small bowl stir together yogurt, cucumber, mayonnaise and dill weed. Season with salt. Cover and refrigerate at least 1 hour.

2   Rinse fish; pat dry with paper towels. In a large skillet bring water and wine to a boil. Gently add fish. Return to a boil; reduce heat. Cover and simmer for 10 to 11 minutes or until fish flakes with a fork (145°F/63°C). Serve with cucumber mixture.

Makes 4 servings

U.S. Per Serving: 276 calories, 4g carbohydrate, 34g protein, 11g fat, 0g fiber, 101mg cholesterol, 185mg sodium, 0g Omega-3
Canada Per Serving: 1156.35 kJ, 33.67g protein, 11.25g fat, 3.66g carbohydrate, 0.12g dietary fibre, 185.06mg sodium, 578.24mg potassium, 0.32g Omega-3

grilled haddock with orange-chili rub

Prep Time: 5 minutes
Chill Time: 2 hours
Cook Time: 9 minutes

2 (10-oz./284g) fresh or thawed haddock fillets, about ¾ inch thick
3 tbsp. (44ml) brown sugar
1 tbsp. (15ml) finely shredded orange peel
1 tbsp. (15ml) chopped fresh oregano
2 tsp. (10ml) finely shredded lemon peel
1½ tsp. (7.5ml) chili powder
½ tsp. (2.5ml) salt
Lemon wedges or orange wedges

1   Rinse fish; pat dry with paper towels. Cut fish into 4 serving-size pieces.

2   In a small bowl stir together brown sugar, orange peel, oregano, lemon peel, chili powder and salt. Place fish, skin-side down, in a single layer in a shallow dish. Rub sugar mixture over fish. Cover and refrigerate for 2 to 8 hours.

3   Preheat grill to medium. Prepare grill for indirect cooking. Remove fish from the pan, draining off any juices. Place fish, skin-side down, on the grill rack. Grill, covered, for 9 to 13 minutes or until fish flakes when tested with a fork (145°F/63°C). Do not turn fish.

4   Serve with lemon or orange wedges.

Makes 4 servings

U.S. Per Serving: 130 calories, 12g carbohydrate, 18g protein, 1g fat, 1g fiber, 55mg cholesterol, 952mg sodium, 0g Omega-3
Canada Per Serving: 544.35 kJ, 18.41g protein, 0.86g fat, 11.59g carbohydrate, 0.90g dietary fibre, 951.96mg sodium, 371.87mg potassium, 0.19g Omega-3

haddock

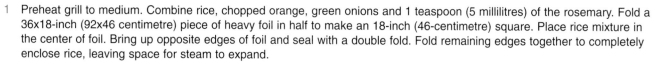

Prep Time: 10 minutes
Cook Time: 25 minutes

2 cups (473ml) cooked rice
1 medium orange or tangerine, peeled and chopped
¼ cup (59ml) sliced green onion
2 tsp. (10ml) chopped fresh rosemary, divided
2 tbsp. (30ml) orange or tangerine juice
1 tsp. (5ml) vegetable oil
⅛ tsp. (.62ml) fresh ground pepper
1 lb. (454g) haddock fillets

1 Preheat grill to medium. Combine rice, chopped orange, green onions and 1 teaspoon (5 millilitres) of the rosemary. Fold a 36x18-inch (92x46 centimetre) piece of heavy foil in half to make an 18-inch (46-centimetre) square. Place rice mixture in the center of foil. Bring up opposite edges of foil and seal with a double fold. Fold remaining edges together to completely enclose rice, leaving space for steam to expand.

2 Place rice packet on grill and cook 15 minutes or until heated through, turning once.

3 Meanwhile, combine orange juice, remaining 1 teaspoon (5 millilitres) rosemary, oil and pepper. Brush on haddock fillets. Place fillets on greased grill rack, tucking under any thin edges.

4 Grill fish for 5 minutes per ½ inch (1.3 centimetre) thickness, turning once (145°F/63°C). Serve with rice.

Makes 4 servings

U.S. Per Serving: 224 calories, 27g carbohydrate, 24g protein, 2g fat, 1g fiber, 130mg cholesterol, 127mg sodium, 0g Omega-3
Canada Per Serving: 938kJ, 23.63g protein, 2.47g fat, 27.48g carbohydrate, 1.34g dietary fibre, 126.96mg sodium, 122.79mg potassium, 0.01g Omega-3

haddock with spicy shrimp sauce

Prep Time: 5 minutes
Cook Time: 25 minutes

2 green onions, thinly sliced
1 clove garlic, chopped
1 tsp. (5ml) olive oil
3 roma tomatoes, chopped
1½ tsp. (7.5ml) chopped jalapeño or serrano pepper
½ cup (118ml) thawed small precooked, peeled and deveined shrimp
4 (4- to 5-oz./113 to 142g) haddock fillets
Hot cooked couscous (optional)

1 Preheat grill to medium. In a saucepan cook onion and garlic in olive oil. Stir in tomatoes, pepper and shrimp. Heat through.

2 Place fish in a shallow foil pan. Top with shrimp mixture. Season to taste with salt and pepper.

3 Arrange grill for indirect cooking. Place foil pan on grill rack. Grill, covered, for 20 to 22 minutes or until fish flakes easily when tested with a fork. Spoon juices over fish. Serve with hot cooked couscous, if desired.

Makes 4 servings

U.S. Per Serving: 133 calories, 3g carbohydrate, 25g protein, 3g fat, 1g fiber, 48mg cholesterol, 165mg sodium, 0g Omega-3
Canada Per Serving: 555.77 kJ, 25.30g protein, 2.66g fat, 3.17g carbohydrate, 0.76g dietary fibre, 165.12mg sodium, 160.54mg potassium, 0.09g Omega-3

halibut

The Latin name for Halibut means (loosely) "hippo." It is the largest of the flatfish, sometimes attaining weights of 500 pounds (226.8kg), although more common market weights range between 50 and 100 pounds (22.7 to 45.4kg).

SOURCE: Halibut live near the bottom of cold, clear ocean water. They are harvested along the northern coastlines of both the Atlantic and Pacific oceans with the most halibut coming from Alaskan waters. Available year around, the greatest supply is from March to September.

SELECTION & HANDLING: Pacific halibut are often cut into fletches—quartered sections of the fish that have no bones and can weigh up to 10 pounds (4.5kg) each. Fresh or frozen halibut steaks and fillets are also available. Near harvesting areas, look for halibut cheeks. The texture is crab-like and the flavor is particularly sweet.

FLAVOR: Mild and sweet.

FLESH: Dense and tender with a firm flake.

PREPARATION: Halibut may be grilled, broiled, roasted or sautéed. However, due to its tendency to dry out, it's best when cooked with moist heat such as poaching, braising or steaming.

Prep Time: 20 minutes
Cook Time: 10 minutes

¼ cup (59ml) Dijon-style mustard
¼ cup (59ml) butter or margarine, melted
2 tbsp. (30ml) honey
2 tsp. (10ml) lemon juice
1½ lb. (680g) fresh or thawed halibut steaks, about 1 inch (2.5cm) thick
1 small green bell pepper, cut into 1½-inch (3.8cm) pieces
1 small yellow bell pepper, cut into 1½-inch (3.8cm) pieces
1 small orange bell pepper, cut into 1½-inch (3.8cm) pieces
1 cup grape tomatoes (237ml)
1 small onion, cut into 1½-inch (3.8cm) pieces

1 Preheat the broiler. Lightly coat the rack of a broiler pan with nonstick cooking spray.

2 In a small bowl whisk together mustard, butter, honey and lemon juice. Set aside.

3 Rinse fish; pat dry with paper towels. Cut fish into 1-inch (2.5-centimetre) pieces. On 12 long metal skewers alternately thread fish pieces, peppers, tomatoes and onion, leaving about ⅛-inch (.32-centimetre) space between pieces. Season with salt and pepper.

4 Place skewers on the broiler pan rack. Broil 4 to 5 inches (10 to 13 centimetres) from the heat for 10 to 11 minutes or until fish flakes with a fork (145°F/63°C), turning kabobs once and brushing with mustard mixture during the last 3 to 4 minutes of broiling.

Makes 6 servings

U.S. Per Serving: 242 calories, 9g carbohydrate, 25g protein, 12g fat, 1g fiber, 57mg cholesterol, 123mg sodium, 0g Omega-3
Canada Per Serving: 1012.84 kJ, 25.25g protein, 11.5g fat, 9.45g carbohydrate, 1.32g dietary fibre, 122.72mg sodium, 162.18mg potassium, 0.02g Omega-3

honey & mustard halibut skewers

broiled halibut with tomato & dill

Prep Time: 15 minutes
Cook Time: 10 minutes

1 lb. (454g) fresh or thawed halibut fillets, about 1 inch (2.5cm) thick
1 tbsp. (15ml) olive oil
½ cup (118ml) sliced green onions
1 tbsp. (15ml) olive oil
2 cups (473ml) cherry tomatoes, halved
2 tbsp. (30ml) chopped fresh dill weed

1 Preheat the broiler. Rinse fish; pat dry with paper towels. Brush halibut with 1 tablespoon (15 millilitres) of the olive oil. Season with salt and pepper. Place on a broiler pan rack.

2 Broil 4 to 5 inches (10 to 13 centimetres) from the heat for 10 to 11 minutes or until fish flakes with a fork (145°F/63°C), turning once.

3 Meanwhile, in a skillet cook green onions in remaining 1 tablespoon (15 millilitres) olive oil until tender. Stir in tomatoes and dill weed. Cook and stir just until tomatoes are soft. Season with salt and pepper.

4 Spoon tomato mixture over halibut.

Makes 4 servings

U.S. Per Serving: 205 calories, 4g carbohydrate, 25g protein, 10g fat, 1g fiber, 37mg cholesterol, 71mg sodium, 0g Omega-3
Canada Per Serving: 859.87 kJ, 24.69g protein, 9.90g fat, 4.39g carbohydrate, 1.15g dietary fibre, 70.59mg sodium, 201.94mg potassium, 0g Omega-3

lobster

Northern or American ("Maine") lobster are distinguished from the spiny or rock lobster by a set of claws, one large crusher claw and a smaller one used to hold prey. The black lobsters with dark brown, red or green hues are closely related to European lobsters. They can live to an old age and weigh up to 45 pounds (20kg), but most are sold at 1 to 5 pounds (454g to 2.3kg).

SOURCE: The lobsters thrive in cold waters of the North Atlantic. They are caught in traps from Labrador down to Virginia, although most come from coastal waters of Canada, Massachusetts and Maine.

SELECTION & HANDLING: Sold live, frozen, raw or cooked, in shell or out, whole and as picked meat. When choosing live lobsters, look for lively ones. Refrigerate live lobsters in moist packaging such as seaweed or damp paper strips or drape with a moist cloth for up to 24 hours. Do not place them in airtight containers, water or salt water.

FLAVOR: Distinctively sweet.

FLESH: Firm, tender, snowy white with red tinges when cooked.

PREPARATION: Lobsters are best when simply steamed or boiled. During cooking, greenish-blue live lobsters turn bright red. Large (greater than 3 pounds/1.4kg) or old lobsters can be just as tender and flavorful as small lobsters. Toughness results from overcooking.

Prep Time: 15 minutes
Cook Time: 4 minutes
Chill Time: 2 hours

3 (6-oz./170g) fresh or thawed lobster tails
⅓ cup (79ml) dry white wine
¼ cup (59ml) lime juice
1 tbsp. (15ml) olive oil
1 tsp. (5ml) finely shredded lime peel
6 leaves butter or Boston lettuce

1   Rinse lobster tails; pat dry with paper towels. Use kitchen scissors to cut through hard top shell of lobster tail. Remove meat. Cut lobster meat into bite-size pieces.

2   In a wok or large skillet combine wine, lime juice, olive oil and lime peel. Bring to a boil; reduce heat. Simmer, uncovered, for 2 minutes. Stir in lobster. Return to a boil; reduce heat. Simmer, uncovered, for 2 to 4 minutes or until lobster is opaque. Transfer to a bowl. Cover and refrigerate at least 2 hours or until well chilled.

3   Place lettuce leaves in small bowls. Top with lobster mixture.

Makes 6 appetizer servings

U.S. Per Serving: 109 calories, 2g carbohydrate, 16g protein, 3g fat, 0g fiber, 81mg cholesterol, 253mg sodium, 0g Omega-3
Canada Per Serving: 457 kJ, 16.14g protein, 3.13g fat, 1.63g carbohydrate, 0.12g dietary fibre, 252.73mg sodium, 274.70mg potassium, 0.01g Omega-3

lobster tails with lime butter

Prep Time: 15 minutes
Cook Time: 6 minutes

4 (6-oz./170g) fresh or thawed lobster tails
2 tbsp. (30ml) butter or margarine, melted
2 tbsp. (30ml) lime juice
1 tbsp. (15ml) olive oil
¼ tsp. (1ml) paprika

1   Rinse lobster tails; pat dry with paper towels. Use kitchen scissors to cut through hard top shell of lobster tail, cutting through meat, but not through the lower shell. Spread meat open in shell. Preheat the broiler.

2   In a small bowl whisk together butter, lime juice, olive oil and paprika.

3   Place lobster tails, meat-side up, on the broiler pan rack. Set aside 3 tablespoons (44 millilitres) of butter mixture; keep warm. Brush lobster meat with remaining butter mixture.

4   Broil 4 to 5 inches (10 to 13 centimetres) from heat for 6 to 8 minutes or until opaque in the center. Drizzle with reserved butter mixture.

Makes 4 servings

U.S. Per Serving: 275 calories, 5g carbohydrate, 35g protein, 12g fat, 0g fiber, 134mg cholesterol, 301mg sodium, 1g Omega-3
Canada Per Serving: 1152.76 kJ, 35.07g protein, 12.09g fat, 4.90g carbohydrate, 0.06g dietary fibre, 301.02mg sodium, 317.46mg potassium, 0.65g Omega-3

lobster

Prep Time: 28 minutes
Cook Time: 30 minutes

2 (1¼- to 1½-lb./567 to 680g) live lobsters
¼ cup (59ml) butter or margarine
2 tbsp. (30ml) lemon juice
1 tbsp. (15ml) finely shredded lemon peel
2 tsp. (10ml) chopped fresh tarragon
2 tsp. (10ml) chopped fresh chives
¾ cup (178ml) fresh bread crumbs (1 slice)

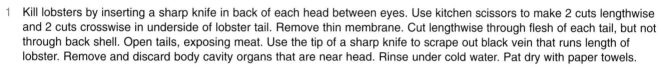

1 Kill lobsters by inserting a sharp knife in back of each head between eyes. Use kitchen scissors to make 2 cuts lengthwise and 2 cuts crosswise in underside of lobster tail. Remove thin membrane. Cut lengthwise through flesh of each tail, but not through back shell. Open tails, exposing meat. Use the tip of a sharp knife to scrape out black vein that runs length of lobster. Remove and discard body cavity organs that are near head. Rinse under cold water. Pat dry with paper towels.

2 Lightly coat the grill rack with nonstick cooking spray. Preheat the grill to medium. Prepare grill for indirect cooking.

3 In a small saucepan cook and stir butter, lemon juice, lemon peel, tarragon and chives over low heat until butter is melted.

4 Place lobsters, shell-side down, on the grill rack. Brush generously with some butter mixture. Grill, covered, for 20 to 30 minutes or until lobster meat is nearly opaque, brushing twice with butter mixture. Do not turn lobsters. Sprinkle with bread crumbs and drizzle with remaining butter mixture. Cover and grill for 10 to 12 minutes more or until lobster meat is opaque.

Makes 2 servings

U.S. Per Serving: 517 calories, 31g carbohydrate, 34g protein, 28g fat, 2g fiber, 203mg cholesterol, 759mg sodium, 0g Omega-3
Canada Per Serving: 2162.71 kJ, 34.34g protein, 27.62g fat, 31.29g carbohydrate, 1.90g dietary fibre, 759.36mg sodium, 451.97mg potassium, 0g Omega-3

how to crack a cooked lobster

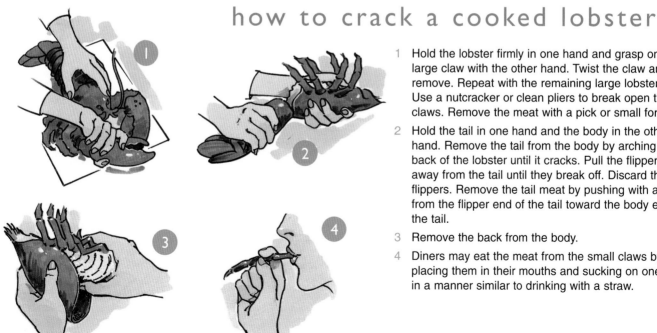

1 Hold the lobster firmly in one hand and grasp one large claw with the other hand. Twist the claw and remove. Repeat with the remaining large lobster claw. Use a nutcracker or clean pliers to break open the claws. Remove the meat with a pick or small fork.

2 Hold the tail in one hand and the body in the other hand. Remove the tail from the body by arching the back of the lobster until it cracks. Pull the flippers away from the tail until they break off. Discard the flippers. Remove the tail meat by pushing with a fork from the flipper end of the tail toward the body end of the tail.

3 Remove the back from the body.

4 Diners may eat the meat from the small claws by placing them in their mouths and sucking on one end in a manner similar to drinking with a straw.

mackerel

Mackerel describes a family of 49 species that includes fish roving in large schools in every ocean and sea of the world. They are lovely with beautiful shapes and colors.

SOURCE: Chub mackerel are the most popular variety and are found in warm waters, along with wahoo mackerel. Atlantic mackerel comes primarily from the mid-Atlantic region of the United States. King mackerel are harvested off South Carolina. Less well-known species, such as Spanish, painted and sierra, are found in the waters of Florida and the Gulf of Mexico.

SELECTION & HANDLING: Since colors fade with age, shop for the most vivid mackerel. Mackerel on ice should appear to be almost alive. Small mackerel (about 1 pound/454g) are sold whole. Larger mackerel are cut into steaks or fillets.

FLAVOR: Full, distinctive.

FLESH: Moderately firm, few bones.

PREPARATION: A relatively high oil content makes mackerel perfect for smoking, broiling and grilling. Smoked mackerel may be cut into bites to serve as an appetizer or stirred into a dip or spread. Upon cooking, the grayish flesh of mackerel firms up and turns off-white.

Prep Time: 15 minutes
Cook Time: 8 minutes

> 1 lb. (454g) fresh or thawed mackerel steaks, about 1 inch (2.5cm) thick
> Dash garlic powder
> 1 tbsp. (15ml) vegetable oil
> ½ medium green bell pepper, cut into julienne strips
> 1 small onion, slivered
> ½ chopped dried hot chile pepper
> ⅓ cup (79ml) cider vinegar

1   Rinse fish; pat dry with paper towels. Cut fish into 1-inch (2.5-centimetre) pieces.
    Sprinkle with garlic powder. Season with salt and pepper.

2   In a wok or large skillet heat oil over high heat. (Add more oil as necessary during cooking.) Add half the fish; stir-fry for
    3 to 5 minutes or until fish flakes with a fork (145°F/63°C). Remove fish. Repeat with remaining fish.

3   Add bell pepper, onion and chile pepper to wok. Stir-fry for 1 to 3 minutes or until crisp-tender. Add vinegar. Bring to a boil.
    Add vegetable mixture to fish, tossing gently until combined.

Makes 6 servings

U.S. Per Serving: 182 calories, 2g carbohydrate, 14g protein, 13g fat, 0g fiber, 53mg cholesterol, 69mg sodium, 2g Omega-3
Canada Per Serving: 762.69 kJ, 14.29g protein, 12.87g fat, 1.75g carbohydrate, 0.40g dietary fibre, 68.63mg sodium, 274.09mg potassium, 1.86g Omega-3

spicy grilled mackerel

Prep Time: 35 minutes
Cook Time: 10 minutes

> 3 medium tomatoes, peeled and chopped
> 1 small onion, chopped
> ⅓ cup (79ml) jalapeño jelly
> 3 tbsp. (44ml) vinegar
> 2 tbsp. (30ml) chopped fresh tarragon
> ½ tsp. (2.5ml) crushed red pepper
> ¼ tsp. (1ml) salt
> 1½ lb. (680g) fresh or thawed mackerel fillets, about 1 inch (2.5cm) thick

1   In a medium saucepan stir together tomatoes, onion, jelly, vinegar, tarragon,
    red pepper and salt. Bring to a boil; reduce heat. Simmer, covered, for
    30 minutes. Cool.

2   Lightly coat the grill rack with nonstick cooking spray. Preheat the grill to medium.

3   Rinse mackerel; pat dry with paper towels. Remove skin. Cut into 4 serving-size
    pieces. Season with salt and pepper. Grill fish for 10 to 12 minutes or until fish
    flakes with a fork (145°F/63°C), turning once.

4   Serve fish topped with tomato mixture.

Makes 4 servings

U.S. Per Serving: 536 calories, 36g carbohydrate, 38g protein, 25g fat, 8g fiber, 119mg cholesterol,
383mg sodium, 4g Omega-3
Canada Per Serving: 2245.05 kJ, 37.94g protein, 25.17g fat, 36.47g carbohydrate,
7.79g dietary fibre, 382.64mg sodium, 766.41mg potassium, 4.19g Omega-3

mahi mahi

Mahi mahi is also known as dorado, dolphin and dolphin-fish, yet it is not a relative to the marine mammal.

SOURCE: Mahi mahi is found in most of the world's warm waters. It is caught throughout the Caribbean, off the shores of Florida, near Hawaii and from southern California to Panama.

SELECTION & HANDLING: The market size of mahi mahi ranges from a few pounds to more than 50 pounds (22.7kg). It is typically sold fresh or frozen as steaks or fillets. Look for consistently colored pink to light beige flesh. Mahi mahi begins to darken and get streaky as it ages.

FLAVOR: Mild and slightly sweet.

FLESH: Firm with large flakes.

PREPARATION: For the mildest flavor, remove the tough skin and cut away the dark lateral line of mahi mahi before cooking. It may be prepared by any cookery method, but lends itself well to grilling and broiling. Flavorful ingredients enhance the mild flavor of mahi mahi.

Prep Time: 10 minutes
Chill Time: 2 hours
Cook Time: 7 minutes

2 medium tomatoes, chopped
2 tbsp. (30ml) lime juice
1 tbsp. (15ml) olive oil
1 tbsp. (15ml) chopped fresh parsley
1 clove garlic, minced
¼ tsp. (1ml) bottled hot pepper sauce
1½ lb. (680g) fresh or thawed mahi mahi steaks, about ¾ inch (1.9cm) thick
1 tbsp. (15ml) olive oil

1   In a small bowl combine tomatoes, lime juice, 1 tablespoon (15 millilitres) of the olive oil, parsley, garlic and hot pepper sauce. Cover and refrigerate for 2 to 12 hours.

2   Preheat the grill to medium. Rinse fish; pat dry with paper towels. Cut into 4 serving-size pieces. Brush fish with remaining 1 tablespoon (15 millilitres) olive oil. Grill fish for 7 to 9 minutes or until fish flakes with a fork (145°F/63°C), turning once. Serve with tomato mixture.

Makes 4 servings

U.S. Per Serving: 222 calories, 4g carbohydrate, 32g protein, 8g fat, 1g fiber, 125mg cholesterol, 159mg sodium, 0g Omega-3

Canada Per Serving: 930.71 kJ, 32.35g protein, 8.42g fat, 4.11g carbohydrate, 0.75g dietary fibre, 159.39mg sodium, 153.19mg potassium, 0g Omega-3

grilled mahi mahi

Prep Time: 10 minutes
Cook Time: 4 minutes

1 cup (237ml) dry red wine
3 tbsp. (44ml) sliced green onions
3 tbsp. (44ml) lime juice
2 tbsp. (30ml) brown sugar
½ tsp. (2.5ml) salt
1 clove garlic, minced
4 (6-oz./170g) fresh or thawed mahi mahi fillets, about ½ inch (1.3cm) thick

1   In a small saucepan combine wine, green onions, lime juice, sugar, salt and garlic. Bring to a boil; reduce heat. Simmer, uncovered, for 5 minutes. Cool.

2   Preheat the grill to medium. Lightly coat a grill basket with nonstick cooking spray.

3   Rinse fish; pat dry with paper towels. Brush fillets with wine mixture. Place fish in the grill basket. Tuck under any thin edges of fish. Grill for 4 to 6 minutes or until fish flakes with a fork (145°F/63°C), brushing with wine mixture frequently.

Makes 4 servings

U.S. Per Serving: 220 calories, 9g carbohydrate, 32g protein, 1g fat, g fiber, 125mg cholesterol, 448mg sodium, 0g Omega-3

Canada Per Serving: 919.80 kJ, 32.02g protein, 1.22g fat, 9.35g carbohydrate, 0.18g dietary fibre, 448.18mg sodium, 118.55mg potassium, 0g Omega-3

ocean perch····

Ocean perch are also called redfish, rosefish, red perch and deep-sea perch and are members of the rockfish family. Most are a brilliant red to orange color, although some perch from the Pacific Ocean may be black or yellow. They have short bodies and large broad heads.

SOURCE: Pacific Ocean perch inhabit the waters from Alaska to Mexico. Atlantic Ocean perch are found in the deep waters of the continental shelf, primarily off Canada's and the New England states' coastlines.

SELECTION & HANDLING: Primarily ocean perch is marketed fresh or frozen as fillets, though it is available whole. Pacific Ocean perch (sometimes called by its initials POP) is usually sold with the skin removed. Atlantic Ocean perch is usually sold with the skin on.

FLAVOR: Pacific Ocean perch have a mild flavor. Atlantic Ocean perch have a slightly more distinctive flavor.

FLESH: Medium-firm with a large flake.

PREPARATION: Both Atlantic and Pacific perch provide excellent table fare and may be cooked by any method. They are excellent baked, broiled or oven-fried.

almond & mushroom topped perch

Prep Time: 20 minutes
Cook Time: 12 minutes

2 lb. (907g) fresh or thawed ocean perch fillets, about ½ inch (1.3cm) thick
1 cup (237ml) milk
1 beaten egg
1 cup (237ml) flour
½ tsp. (2.5ml) salt
2 tbsp. (30ml) vegetable or olive oil
1½ cups (355ml) sliced fresh mushrooms
2 tbsp. (30ml) butter or margarine
½ cup (118ml) chopped smoky-flavored almonds
2 tbsp. (30ml) chopped fresh parsley
1 tbsp. (15ml) lemon juice

1   Rinse fish; pat dry with paper towels. In a shallow dish combine milk and egg. In another shallow dish combine flour and salt. Dip fish into egg mixture, then coat with flour mixture.

2   In a large skillet heat 2 tablespoons (30 millilitres) of the oil. Add half of the fish. Cook over medium-high heat for 5 to 7 minutes or until golden brown and fish flakes with a fork (145°F/63°C), turning once. Drain on paper towels. Repeat with remaining 2 tablespoons (30 millilitres) oil and remaining fish. Keep warm.

3   In a medium saucepan cook mushrooms in butter or margarine until tender. Stir in almonds, parsley and lemon juice. Spoon over fish.

Makes 6 servings

U.S. Per Serving: 489 calories, 22g carbohydrate, 37g protein, 29g fat, 3g fiber, 110mg cholesterol, 451mg sodium, 1g Omega-3
Canada Per Serving: 2047.43 kJ, 37.15g protein, 28.69g fat, 21.92g carbohydrate, 2.68g dietary fibre, 451.04mg sodium, 647.29mg potassium, 0.56g Omega-3

ocean perch with pine nuts

Prep Time: 10 minutes
Cook Time: 5 minutes

¼ cup (59ml) butter or margarine, melted
¼ cup (59ml) pine nuts, toasted
2 tbsp. (30ml) chopped fresh chives
1½ lb. (680g) fresh or thawed ocean perch fillets, about ½ inch (1.3cm) thick
2 lemons, sliced

1   Preheat the grill to medium.

2   In a small bowl stir together butter, pine nuts and chives. Set aside.

3   Rinse fish; pat dry with paper towels. Arrange sliced lemons on the grill rack. Place fish on top of lemon slices. Tuck under any thin pieces of fish. Grill for 5 to 6 minutes or until fish flakes with a fork (145°F/63°C). Carefully transfer fish to a serving plate. Spoon pine nut mixture on top.

Makes 4 servings

U.S. Per Serving: 469 calories, 11g carbohydrate, 41g protein, 32g fat, 4g fiber, 101mg cholesterol, 131mg sodium, 1g Omega-3
Canada Per Serving: 1960.19 kJ, 40.53g protein, 32.18g fat, 10.68g carbohydrate, 4.11g dietary fibre, 130.60mg sodium, 750.77mg potassium, 0.81g Omega-3

orange roughy

Orange roughy have reddish bodies and bluish-tinged bellies that turn bright coral after harvest (hence the name). They average 3 to 4 pounds (1.4 to 1.8kg) each and are about 12 inches (30.5cm) long.

SOURCE: Orange roughy come from the Tasman Sea in the South Pacific and off the coasts of New Zealand, Australia and Chile. They are caught in very deep waters by huge trawl nets.

SELECTION & HANDLING: Orange roughy are most commonly available as fillets. The fish is usually frozen at sea, thawed on land, cut into fillets and refrozen. Despite the fact that orange roughy meat is frozen twice before it gets to retail markets, it holds up extremely well.

FLAVOR: Delicate, shellfish-like.

FLESH: Tender, firm and dense.

PREPARATION: Orange roughy are especially suitable for baking, broiling and sautéeing. Any recipe for flounder or sole may be successfully adapted for orange roughy.

Prep Time: 15 minutes
Cook Time: 7 minutes

1½ lb. (680g) fresh or thawed orange roughy fillets, about ¾ inch (1.9cm) thick
2 medium tomatoes, peeled, seeded and chopped
1 small onion, finely chopped
2 tbsp. (30ml) chopped fresh dill weed
Hot cooked brown rice (optional)

1   Preheat oven to 450°F/232°C. Lightly coat a baking dish with nonstick cooking spray. Rinse fish; pat dry with paper towels. Place fish in the baking dish. Sprinkle with tomatoes, onion and dill weed. Season with salt and pepper.

2   Cover with foil. Bake for 7 to 11 minutes or until fish flakes with a fork (145°F/63°C).

3   Serve with brown rice, if desired.

Makes 4 servings

U.S. Per Serving: 137 calories, 4g carbohydrate, 26g protein, 1g fat, 1g fiber, 34mg cholesterol, 113mg sodium, 0g Omega-3

Canada Per Serving: 574.03 kJ, 25.74g protein, 1.42g fat, 4.38g carbohydrate, 1g dietary fibre, 113.39mg sodium, 676.36mg potassium, 0.01g Omega-3

orange roughy
with herbed citrus sauce

Prep Time: 10 minutes
Cook Time: 4 minutes

2 medium oranges, peeled and finely chopped
3 tbsp. (44ml) mayonnaise
3 tbsp. (44ml) sliced green onions
2 tbsp. (30ml) chopped fresh parsley
2 tsp. (10ml) chopped fresh tarragon or ½ tsp. (2.5ml) dried tarragon, crushed
2 tsp. (10ml) finely shredded lemon peel
4 (6-oz./170g) fresh or thawed orange roughy fillets, about ½ inch (1.3cm) thick
1 tsp. (5ml) olive oil

1   Spray the grill rack with nonstick cooking spray. Preheat the grill to medium.

2   In a small bowl stir together oranges, mayonnaise, green onions, parsley, tarragon and lemon peel. Cover and refrigerate until serving time.

3   Rinse fish; pat dry with paper towels. Brush fish on both sides with oil. Grill fish for 4 to 6 minutes or until fish flakes with a fork (145°F/63°C), turning once.

4   Serve fish with orange mixture.

Makes 4 servings

U.S. Per Serving: 200 calories, 10g carbohydrate, 26g protein, 6g fat, 2g fiber, 38mg cholesterol, 176mg sodium, 0g Omega-3

Canada Per Serving: 835.55 kJ, 25.62g protein, 6.28g fat, 10.29g carbohydrate, 1.87g dietary fibre, 176.38mg sodium, 662.79mg potassium, 0.01g Omega-3

orange roughy

Prep Time: 15 minutes
Cook Time: 7 minutes

¼ cup (59ml) dry white wine
1½ lb. (680g) orange roughy fillets, about ¾ inch (1.9cm) thick
2 tbsp. (30ml) olive oil
2 tbsp. (30ml) chopped fresh basil
2 tbsp. (30ml) finely shredded lemon peel
½ tsp. (2.5ml) freshly ground black pepper

1 Preheat oven to 450°F/232°C. Pour wine into a 13x9x2-inch
(33x23x5-centimetre) baking dish.

2 Rinse fish; pat dry with paper towels. Cut into 4 serving-size pieces. Brush fish on both sides with olive oil. Place in
baking dish.

3 In a small bowl combine basil, lemon peel and pepper. Sprinkle over fish. Cover baking dish with foil. Bake for 7 to
11 minutes or until fish flakes with a fork (145°F/63°C).

4 Carefully transfer fillets to a serving platter. Discard cooking juices.

Makes 4 servings

U.S. Per Serving: 190 calories,1g carbohydrate, 25g protein, 8g fat, 0g fiber, 34mg cholesterol, 108mg sodium, 0g Omega-3
Canada Per Serving: 796.78 kJ, 25.12g protein, 8.23g fat, 0.84g carbohydrate, 0.39g dietary fibre, 108.26mg sodium, 533.02mg potassium,
0.01g Omega-3

citrus poached orange roughy

Prep Time: 10 minutes
Cook Time: 7 minutes

1½ lb. (680g) fresh or thawed orange roughy fillets, about ¾ inch (1.9cm) thick
1 cup (237ml) orange juice
½ cup (118ml) water
¼ cup (59ml) dry white wine
4 tsp. (20ml) butter or margarine, melted
2 tsp. (10ml) chopped fresh cilantro
4 orange slices
4 lime slices
4 lemon slices

1 Rinse fish; pat dry with paper towels. Cut fish into 4 serving-size pieces.

2 In a large skillet combine orange juice, water and wine. Bring to a boil.
Carefully add fish pieces. Return to a boil; reduce heat. Cover and simmer for
7 to 9 minutes or until fish flakes with a fork (145°F/63°C). Transfer fish to a
warm serving platter.

3 Meanwhile, in a small bowl stir together butter and cilantro. Drizzle over fish.

4 Garnish with orange, lime and lemon slices.

Makes 4 servings

U.S. Per Serving: 190 calories, 7g carbohydrate, 25g protein, 5g fat, 0g fiber, 44mg cholesterol,
109mg sodium, 0g Omega-3
Canada Per Serving: 796.78 kJ, 25.46g protein, 5.32g fat, 6.57g carbohydrate,
0.13g dietary fibre, 108.60mg sodium, 646.97mg potassium, 0.01g Omega-3

salmon

There are many varieties of salmon, with all but one coming from the Pacific Ocean. That one is primarily farm-raised and is known as the Atlantic salmon or is named for its country of origin. The Pacific salmon include king, chum, coho and sockeye.

SOURCE: Atlantic salmon are farm-raised in a dozen countries including the United States, United Kingdom, Chile, Norway, Canada, Ireland and Iceland. Chum salmon have wide distribution in the Pacific Ocean. Cohos are found in coastal streams from California to Alaska, as well as in Japan and Korea. Sockeye salmon are found in the Pacific Ocean off the coasts of North America and Asia.

SELECTION & HANDLING: Salmon are sold fresh or frozen as whole fish, dressed fish, fillets and steaks. Some Atlantic salmon are available as patties, hams and kabobs. Fresh or thawed salmon should be used within 1 to 2 days.

FLAVOR: Mild.

FLESH: Moderately firm and moist with colors ranging from pink to deep red.

PREPARATION: Salmon steaks, fillets and whole fish may be baked, broiled, poached or grilled.

salmon & pineapple with gingered teriyaki sauce

Prep Time: 10 minutes
Cook Time: 10 minutes

2 tbsp. (30ml) bottled teriyaki sauce
1 tsp. (5ml) grated fresh gingerroot or ¼ tsp. (1ml) ground ginger
1 tsp. (5ml) chopped fresh cilantro
1½ lb. (680g) salmon fillet, about 1 inch (2.5cm) thick
4 (1-inch/2.5cm thick) slices fresh pineapple, cut in half
3 cups (710ml) hot cooked rice
2 tsp. (10ml) chopped fresh cilantro

1   Preheat oven to 450°F/232°C. Lightly coat a large shallow baking pan with nonstick cooking spray.

2   In a small bowl combine teriyaki sauce, gingerroot and 1 teaspoon (5 millilitres) of the cilantro.

3   Rinse fish; pat dry with paper towels. Cut into 4 serving-size pieces. Place salmon and pineapple in the baking pan. Brush with teriyaki mixture.

4   Bake, uncovered, for 10 to 12 minutes or until fish flakes with a fork (145°F/63°C).

5   Stir together rice and remaining 2 teaspoons (10 millilitres) cilantro. Serve with salmon and pineapple.

Makes 4 servings

U.S. Per Serving: 407 calories, 45g carbohydrate, 38g protein, 7g fat, 2g fiber, 127mg cholesterol, 160mg sodium, 0g Omega-3
Canada Per Serving: 1703.99 kJ, 38.17g protein, 7.22g fat, 45.26g carbohydrate, 1.60g dietary fibre, 160.5mg sodium, 139.77mg potassium, 0.07g Omega-3

salmon with tomatoes & chives

Prep Time: 15 minutes
Cook Time: 10 minutes

1 clove garlic, minced
1 tbsp. (15ml) olive oil
¼ cup (59ml) dry white wine
1 medium tomato, chopped
2 tbsp. (30ml) chopped fresh chives
2 tbsp. (30ml) lemon juice
1½ lb. (680kg) fresh or thawed salmon fillet, about 1 inch (1.3cm) thick

1   Lightly coat the grill rack with nonstick cooking spray. Preheat the grill to medium.

2   In a small saucepan cook garlic in olive oil until tender. Carefully stir in wine. Bring to a boil; reduce heat. Simmer, uncovered, for 2 to 3 minutes or until wine is reduced by half. Stir in tomato, chives and lemon juice. Set aside.

3   Rinse fish; pat dry with paper towels. Cut fish into 4 serving-size pieces. Grill salmon fillets for 10 to 11 minutes or until fish flakes with a fork (145°F/63°C), turning once. Serve with warm tomato mixture.

Makes 4 servings

U.S. Per Serving: 256 calories, 3g carbohydrate, 35g protein, 10g fat, 0g fiber, 127mg cholesterol, 89mg sodium, 0g Omega-3
Canada Per Serving: 1069.94kJ, 34.86g protein, 10.13g fat, 2.52g carbohydrate, 0.42g dietary fibre, 89.47mg sodium, 96.97mg potassium, 0g Omega-3

salmon

Prep Time: 15 minutes
Cook Time: 10 minutes

¼ cup (59ml) chopped fresh mint
3 tbsp. (44ml) Dijon-style mustard
3 tbsp. (44ml) white wine vinegar
¾ cup (178ml) olive oil
2 lb. (907g) fresh or thawed salmon fillet, about 1 inch (2.5cm) thick
1 tbsp. (15ml) olive oil

1   In a small mixer bowl combine mint, mustard and vinegar. Beat with an electric mixer on high speed, while slowly adding ¾ cup (178 millilitres) of the olive oil in a thin steady stream. Continue beating until combined.

2   Preheat the grill to medium. Rinse fish; pat dry with paper towels. Remove skin and cut salmon into 6 serving-size pieces. Brush both sides with remaining 1 tablespoon (15 millilitres) olive oil. Grill salmon for 10 to 11 minutes or until fish flakes with a fork (145°F/63°C), turning once.

3   Spoon mustard mixture over hot salmon.

Makes 6 servings

U.S. Per Serving: 456 calories, 1g carbohydrate, 31g protein, 37g fat, 0g fiber, 113mg cholesterol, 120mg sodium, 0g Omega-3
Canada Per Serving: 1907.96 kJ, 31.15g protein, 36.70g fat, 1.01g carbohydrate, 0.22g dietary fibre, 119.61mg sodium, 25.79mg potassium, 0g Omega-3

salmon with tropical salsa

Prep Time: 20 minutes
Cook Time: 7 minutes

2 peaches or mangos, seeded, peeled and chopped
1 large tomato, chopped and drained
½ cup (118ml) sliced green onions
2 tbsp. (30ml) chopped fresh cilantro
1 tbsp. (15ml) balsamic vinegar
2 tsp. (10ml) grated gingerroot or ½ tsp. (2.5ml) ground ginger
4 (6-oz./170g) salmon steaks, about ¾ inch (1.9cm) thick
2 tbsp. (30ml) lemon juice

1   Lightly coat the grill rack with nonstick cooking spray. Preheat the grill to medium.

2   In a medium bowl stir together peaches, tomato, green onions, cilantro, vinegar and gingerroot. Set aside.

3   Rinse fish; pat dry with paper towels. Sprinkle with lemon juice. Grill for 7 to 9 minutes or until fish flakes easily (145°F/63°C), turning once. Serve with peach mixture.

Makes 4 servings

U.S. Per Serving: 246 calories, 10g carbohydrate, 35g protein, 7g fat, 2g fiber, 127mg cholesterol, 92mg sodium, 0g Omega-3
Canada Per Serving: 1027.53 kJ, 35.47g protein, 6.74g fat, 9.80g carbohydrate, 1.87g dietary fibre, 92.25mg sodium, 248.25mg potassium, 0g Omega-3

salmon

salmon with creamy horseradish sauce

Prep Time: 5 minutes
Cook Time: 8 minutes

1½ lb. (680g) fresh or thawed salmon fillet, cut 1 inch (2.5cm) thick
3 tbsp. (44ml) light mayonnaise
2 tsp. (10ml) chopped fresh parsley
1½ tsp. (7.5ml) Dijon mustard
½ to 1 tsp. (2.5 to 5ml) prepared horseradish

1 Rinse fish; pat dry. Combine mayonnaise, parsley, mustard and horseradish; set aside.

2 Spray grill with nonstick cooking spray. Preheat grill to medium. Grill salmon, uncovered, for 5 minutes per ½ inch (1.3 centimetres) of thickness or until fish flakes easily with a fork (145°F/63°C), turning once. Spread horseradish mixture over salmon after turning.

Makes 4 servings

U.S. Per Serving: 352 calories, 2g carbohydrate, 34g protein, 22g fat, 0g fiber, 104mg cholesterol, 181mg sodium, 3g Omega-3

Canada Per Serving: 1472.12 kJ, 34g protein, 22.36g fat, 1.81g carbohydrate, 0.08g dietary fibre, 180.83mg sodium, 631.64mg potassium, 3.41g Omega-3

smoked salmon spread

Prep Time: 10 minutes
Cook Time: 20 minutes

1 (8-oz./227g) pkg. cream cheese, softened
½ cup (118ml) smoky Cheddar cold pack cheese food, softened, or 1 cup (237ml) shredded smoked Cheddar cheese (4 oz./113g), softened
½ cup (118ml) dairy sour cream
1 tsp. (5ml) Worcestershire sauce
1 cup (237ml) skinned and flaked hot-smoked salmon
⅓ cup (79ml) sliced green onions
⅓ cup (79ml) chopped red or green bell pepper
1 tbsp. (15ml) chopped fresh dill weed or ½ tsp. (2.5ml) dried dill weed
Bagel chips or crackers

1 Preheat oven to 350°F/177°C.

2 In a small mixer bowl combine cream cheese, cheese food, sour cream and Worcestershire sauce. Beat with an electric mixer on medium speed until light and fluffy. Stir in salmon, onions, pepper and dill.

3 Spoon into an 8- or 9-inch (20- or 23-centimetre) quiche dish or pie plate. Bake for 20 minutes or until heated through.

4 Transfer dip to serving dish, if desired. Garnish with additional sour cream, green onion and red pepper, if desired. Serve with bagel chips or crackers.

Makes 12 appetizer servings

U.S. Per Serving: 145 calories, 2g carbohydrate, 6g protein, 12g fat, 0g fiber, 41mg cholesterol, 209mg sodium, 0g Omega-3

Canada Per Serving: 607.26 kJ, 5.70g protein, 12.21g fat, 1.52g carbohydrate, 0.16g dietary fibre, 208.99mg sodium, 62.56mg potassium, 0.09g Omega-3

scallops

Many species of scallops are usually classified into two broad groups—bay scallops and sea scallops. Tiny bay scallops only measure ½ inch (1.3cm) in diameter. They are more tender and more expensive than sea scallops. The larger sea scallops are more widely available.

SOURCE: Bay scallops are found in shallow waters from Canada to North Carolina. Increasing numbers are being farm-raised in Nova Scotia and New England. Sea scallops are also found from Newfoundland to North Carolina, as well as in the Pacific Ocean from Alaska to Oregon.

SELECTION & HANDLING: Bay scallops average 70 to 100 scallops per pound (454g) and are usually sold fresh. Sea scallops average 30 per pound (454g) and are sold fresh or frozen. Use fresh or thawed scallops within 2 days and store them as close to 32°F/0°C as possible. Avoid scallops that look artificially shiny, opaque or flabby.

FLAVOR: Distinctively sweet.

FLESH: Cork-shaped, firm and white.

PREPARATION: Scallops may be baked, steamed, poached, broiled, fried or stir-fried until they are opaque. Check for doneness by breaking one in half. Overcooking yields tough scallops.

citrus ginger scallops

Prep Time: 40 minutes
Cook Time: 5 minutes

4 12-inch (30cm) wooden skewers
1 tsp. (5ml) grated orange peel
½ cup (118ml) orange juice
1 tsp. (15ml) grated gingerroot
2 tbsp. (30ml soy sauce
1 clove garlic, minced
1 lb. (454g) sea scallops

1. Soak skewers in water. Stir together peel, juice, ginger, soy sauce and garlic. Pour over scallops. Cover and refrigerate for 30 minutes.
2. Preheat grill to medium-high heat.
3. Drain scallops. Thread onto skewers.
4. Grill for 2 to 2½ minutes. Turn and cook 2 to 2½ minutes longer.

Makes 4 servings

U.S. Per Serving: 120 calories, 7g carbohydrate, 19g protein, 1g fat, 0g fiber, 40mg cholesterol, 380mg sodium, 0g Omega-3
Canada Per Serving: 503.55 kJ, 18.69g protein, 1.07g fat, 7.16g carbohydrate, 0.14g dietary fibre, 379.54mg sodium, 88.59mg potassium, 0.00g Omega-3

scallops with thyme & veggies

Prep Time: 15 minutes
Cook Time: 10 minutes

1 lb. (454g) fresh or thawed
   bay scallops
1 cup (237ml) boiling water
¾ cup (178ml) uncooked couscous
1 tbsp. (15ml) olive oil
¼ tsp. (1ml) salt

¼ tsp. (1ml) pepper
1 small zucchini, halved lengthwise
   and very thinly sliced
¼ cup finely chopped onion
4 tsp. (20ml) chopped fresh thyme
4 plum tomatoes, sliced

1. Preheat the grill to medium.
2. Rinse scallops; pat dry with paper towels. In a small bowl stir together boiling water, couscous, olive oil, salt and pepper. Stir in scallops, zucchini, onion and thyme.
3. Tear four 36x18-inch (91x46-centimetre) pieces of heavy foil. Fold each in half to make an 18-inch (46-centimetre) square. Lightly coat each square of foil with nonstick cooking spray.
4. Place one sliced tomato on each foil square. Evenly spoon scallop mixture on top of tomatoes. Bring up opposite edges of foil; seal with a double fold. Fold remaining edges together to completely enclose food, leaving space for steam to expand.
5. Grill packets, covered, for 10 minutes or until scallops are opaque. Open packets carefully.

Makes 4 servings

U.S. Per Serving: 265 calories, 30g carbohydrate, 22g protein, 5g fat, 3g fiber, 0mg cholesterol, 155mg sodium, 0g Omega-3
Canada Per Serving: 1108.36 kJ, 21.98g protein, 4.66g fat, 29.98g carbohydrate, 2.97g dietary fibre, 155.42mg sodium, 286.80mg potassium, 0.01g Omega-3

sea bass

Sea bass, also known as black sea bass, rock bass or blackfish, have small, stout bodies with smoky gray, brown or bluish-black skin. Their scales have pale blue or white centers.

SOURCE: Sea bass are found along the entire Atlantic coast of North America and into the Gulf of Mexico. They're most often found on rocky bottoms near pilings, wrecks and jetties.

SELECTION & HANDLING: Black sea bass tend to be about 10 inches (25.4cm) long and range from 1½ to 3¼ pounds (680g to 1.5kg). Usually they're sold whole but may also be found as fillets. If the fish is bought whole, its spiny, spiky dorsal fin should be carefully removed to avoid injury.

FLAVOR: Very delicate, derived from feeding chiefly on shrimp and crabs.

FLESH: Firm with very white flesh.

PREPARATION: Sea bass can be prepared in a variety of ways including frying, baking, broiling, grilling, steaming or sautéing.

smoked sea bass

Prep Time: 10 minutes
Cook Time: 10 minutes

2 cups (473ml) hickory wood chips or apple wood chips*
2 medium sweet potatoes
2 tbsp. (30ml) vegetable oil
1¼ lb. (567g) sea bass fillets (about 1 inch/2.5cm thick)
1 tbsp. (15ml) Jamaican jerk or Cajun seasoning

1 Soak and use wood chips according to package directions.

2 Preheat grill to medium. Cut sweet potatoes lengthwise into ¼-inch (.64-centimetre) thick slices. Brush with 1 tablespoon (15 millilitres) of the oil. Sprinkle lightly with salt. Brush sea bass with remaining oil and sprinkle with jerk seasoning.

3 Place wood chips in grill according to package directions. Grill potato slices and fish for 10 to 12 minutes, turning once, or until fish flakes easily with a fork (145°F/63°C) and potatoes are crisp-tender.

Makes 4 servings

*Wood chips or chunks add a unique flavor to grilled foods. Always use chips or chunks according to package directions. Experiment with chips such as mesquite, maple and pecan; but never use woods such as pine or spruce.

U.S. Per Serving: 266 calories, 16g carbohydrate, 27g protein, 10g fat, 2g fiber, 58mg cholesterol, 510mg sodium, 1g Omega-3
Canada Per Serving: 1111.90 kJ, 27.20g protein, 10.03g fat, 15.78g carbohydrate, 1.95g dietary fibre, 509.84mg sodium, 495.48mg potassium, 0.86g Omega-3

sea bass with ginger

Prep Time: 20 minutes
Cook Time: 15 minutes

1 small zucchini, cut into julienne strips
1 small yellow summer squash, cut into julienne strips
1 small carrot, cut into julienne strips
1 tbsp. (15ml) grated gingerroot
1 clove garlic, minced
4 (6-oz./170g) fresh or thawed sea bass fillets
4 tsp. (20ml) lemon juice

1 Preheat the grill to medium.

2 Tear four 36x18-inch (91x46-centimetre) pieces of heavy foil. Fold each in half to make an 18-inch (46-centimetre) square. Lightly coat each square of foil with nonstick cooking spray.

3 Toss together zucchini, summer squash, carrot, gingerroot and garlic. Evenly spoon vegetable mixture on foil squares.

4 Rinse fish; pat dry with paper towels. Top vegetables with fish fillets. Sprinkle with lemon juice. Season with salt and pepper. Bring up opposite edges of foil; seal with a double fold. Fold remaining edges together to completely enclose food, leaving space for steam to expand.

5 Grill packets, covered, for 15 to 20 minutes or until fish flakes with a fork (145°F/63°C). Open packets carefully.

Makes 4 servings

U.S. Per Serving: 184 calories, 4g carbohydrate, 32g protein, 4g fat, 1g fiber, 70mg cholesterol, 122mg sodium, 1g Omega-3
Canada Per Serving: 769.23 kJ, 32.24g protein, 3.54g fat, 4.32g carbohydrate, 1.36g dietary fibre, 121.82mg sodium, 621.80mg potassium, 1.04g Omega-3

shrimp

More than 200 species of shrimp come in a variety of colors including red, brown, pink, gray, yellow and off-white. As long as the size of the shrimp is appropriate, most species can be substituted for each other in recipes.

SOURCE: Shrimp come from oceans all over the world and are farm-raised.

SELECTION & HANDLING: Shrimp are sized according to the number per pound (454g). Generally the larger the shrimp, the higher the price. Shrimp in the shell without the head (and sometimes without the legs) are sold both fresh and frozen. Peeled and deveined raw shrimp may be also be purchased fresh or frozen. Ready-to-serve cooked shrimp and frozen cooked shrimp are sold in most markets.

FLAVOR: Mild and sweet.

FLESH: Firm.

PREPARATION: Frozen, precooked shrimp need only to be thawed and rinsed before using. If using raw shrimp, peel and devein them before cooking. Although the sand vein (the dark vein running the length of the shrimp) is safe to eat and tasteless, it may be gritty and should be removed (deveining). Very large shrimp may be butterflied prior to preparation. Shrimp are especially suited for boiling, frying, stir-frying and grilling. Cooked shrimp make great additions to appetizers or salads.

shrimp & vegetable kabobs

Prep Time: 30 minutes
Marinate Time: 1 hour
Cook Time: 12 minutes

1½ lb. (680g) unpeeled,
    large fresh shrimp
1 yellow bell pepper,
    cut into 1½-inch (3.8cm) pieces
1 green bell pepper, cut into
    1½-inch (3.8cm) pieces
1 purple onion, cut into 1-inch (2.5cm) slices
1 pint (473ml) cherry tomatoes

½ cup (118ml) lime juice
¼ cup (59ml) olive oil
2 tbsp. (30ml) honey
2 cloves garlic, minced
¼ cup (59ml) chopped fresh
    cilantro
¼ tsp. (1ml) freshly ground
    pepper

1   Peel shrimp, leaving tails intact; devein, if desired. If using wooden skewers, first soak them in water for 30 minutes. Alternately thread shrimp, peppers, purple onion and cherry tomatoes onto skewers, leaving a ½-inch (1.3 centimetres) space between them. Place in a large shallow dish or heavy-duty, resealable plastic bag.

2   Whisk together lime juice, oil, honey, garlic, cilantro and ground pepper in a small bowl. Pour mixture over kabobs; cover or seal and refrigerate 1 hour, turning occasionally.

3   Remove shrimp kabobs from marinade, discarding marinade.

4   Grill, covered with grill lid, on medium-high 5 minutes or until shrimp turn pink, turning kabobs once. Serve immediately.

Makes 4 to 6 servings

U.S. Per Serving: 388 calories, 24g carbohydrate, 37g protein, 17g fat, 2g fiber, 259mg cholesterol, 262mg sodium, 1g Omega-3
Canada Per Serving: 1625.17 kJ, 36.51g protein, 17.43g fat, 23.61g carbohydrate, 2.48g dietary fibre, 261.83mg sodium, 720.83mg potassium, 0.85g Omega-3

shrimp tacos with avocado salsa

Prep Time: 20 minutes
Cook Time: 8 minutes

1 lb. (454g) large fresh or
    thawed shrimp in shells
¾ tsp. (4ml) chili powder

4 fat-free flour tortillas
1⅓ cups (316ml) shredded lettuce
Avocado Salsa (recipe below)

1   Peel and devein shrimp, removing tails. Rinse shrimp; pat dry. Sprinkle chili powder over shrimp; rub into shrimp. Thread shrimp onto 4 long metal skewers.

2   Preheat grill to medium. Stack tortillas and wrap in foil. Grill shrimp and tortillas, uncovered, until shrimp are opaque and tortillas are heated through, turning shrimp once. Allow 8 to 10 minutes for shrimp and about 5 minutes for tortillas.

3   Remove shrimp from skewers. Immediately fill warm tortillas with lettuce and shrimp. Serve with Avocado Salsa.

Avocado Salsa: Combine ¾ cup (178ml) bottled cilantro-flavored salsa, ½ cup (118ml) chopped avocado and ¼ cup (59ml) peeled, finely chopped jicama. Makes about 1½ cups (355ml).

Makes 4 servings

U.S. Per Serving: 233 calories, 20g carbohydrate, 26g protein, 5g fat, 8g fiber, 172mg cholesterol, 500mg sodium, 1g Omega-3
Canada Per Serving: 976.94 kJ, 26.49g protein, 4.92g fat, 20.07g carbohydrate, 8.47g dietary fibre, 499.68mg sodium, 407.38mg potassium, 0.59g Omega-3

shrimp

Prep Time: 30 minutes
Cook Time: 3 minutes

1 (14½-oz./411g) can diced tomatoes
1 (6¾-oz./191g) pkg. regular Spanish-style rice mix
8 oz. (227g) fresh or thawed shrimp, peeled and deveined
4 cups (.95l) sliced yellow onions
1 green bell pepper, sliced
2 tbsp. (30ml) olive oil
8 cloves garlic, minced
2 cups (473ml) thawed peas
1 tbsp. (15ml) lemon juice

1   In a medium saucepan prepare undrained tomatoes and rice mix according to rice package directions.

2   Meanwhile, rinse shrimp; pat dry with paper towels. In a 12-inch (30-centimetre) skillet cook onions and pepper in hot oil over medium heat until tender, stirring frequently. Stir in shrimp and garlic. Cook and stir for 3 to 4 minutes or until shrimp turn opaque.

3   Stir hot rice mixture, peas and lemon juice into shrimp mixture.

Makes 4 servings

U.S. Per Serving: 453calories, 65g carbohydrate, 22g protein, 13g fat, 8g fiber, 100mg cholesterol, 1223mg sodium, 0g Omega-3
Canada Per Serving: 1895.45 kJ, 21.65g protein, 12.95g fat, 64.84g carbohydrate, 8.27g dietary fibre, 1222.61mg sodium, 366.04mg potassium, 0.29g Omega-3

seafood bisque

Prep Time: 20 minutes
Cook time: 7 minutes

1 (11-oz./312g) can condensed tomato bisque soup or
    one (10¾-oz./305g) can condensed tomato soup
1 cup (237ml) half-and-half or whole milk
8 oz. (227g) cooked shrimp, crab meat and/or lobster meat, cut up
1 tbsp. (15ml) lemon juice
1 tbsp. (15ml) chopped fresh chives
2 tbsp. (30ml) dry sherry (optional)
2 tsp. (10ml) chopped fresh chives

1   In a medium saucepan stir together soup and half-and-half. Cook, stirring often, over medium heat for 5 to 6 minutes or until very hot, but not boiling.

2   Stir in seafood, lemon juice and 1 tablespoon (15 millilitres) of the chives. Stir in sherry, if desired. Cook and stir for 2 to 4 minutes or until heated through.

3   Ladle into serving bowls. Sprinkle with remaining 2 teaspoons (10 millilitres) chives.

Makes 4 servings

U.S. Per Serving: 180 calories, 19g carbohydrate, 15g protein, 5g fat, 1g fiber, 53mg cholesterol, 815mg sodium, 0g Omega-3
Canada Per Serving: 752.32 kJ, 14.89g protein, 4.57g fat, 18.61g carbohydrate, 0.68g dietary fibre, 815.22mg sodium, 289.60mg potassium, 0g Omega-3

shrimp

Prep Time: 20 minutes
Cook Time: 8 minutes

12 oz. (340g) fresh or thawed extra large shrimp, peeled and deveined
1 medium yellow summer squash, sliced
1 medium zucchini, sliced
⅓ cup (79ml) purchased pesto
6 oz. (170g) dried angel hair pasta

1 Preheat the grill to medium.

2 Tear off one 36x18-inch (91x46-centimetre) piece of heavy foil. Lightly coat foil with nonstick cooking spray. Rinse shrimp; pat dry with paper towels. Place shrimp, summer squash and zucchini in center of foil. Spoon pesto evenly over all. Bring up opposite edges of foil; seal with a double fold. Fold remaining edges together to completely enclose food, leaving space for steam to expand.

3 Grill packet for 8 to 10 minutes or until shrimp are opaque and squash is just tender.

4 Meanwhile, cook pasta according to package directions. Drain and keep warm. Toss hot cooked pasta with shrimp and squash mixture.

Makes 4 servings

U.S. Per Serving: 368 calories, 37g carbohydrate, 26g protein, 12g fat, 3g fiber, 133mg cholesterol, 279mg sodium, 0g Omega-3
Canada Per Serving: 1539.02 kJ, 25.67g protein, 12.39g fat, 36.74g carbohydrate, 3.02g dietary fibre, 278.74mg sodium, 374.41mg potassium, 0.46g Omega-3

shrimp & scallop salad with mango dressing

Prep Time: 10 minutes
Cook Time: 5 minutes

⅓ cup (79ml) purchased mango chutney
2 tbsp. (30ml) mayonnaise
2 tbsp. (30ml) orange juice
12 oz. (340g) fresh or thawed large shrimp, peeled and deveined
8 oz. (227g) fresh or thawed sea scallops
6 cups (1.5l) assorted torn greens
2 peaches, seeded, peeled and sliced, or 2 nectarines, seeded and sliced
2 cups (473ml) red or green seedless grapes and/or melon cubes

1 Lightly coat the grill rack with nonstick cooking spray. Preheat the grill to medium.

2 In a small bowl stir together chutney, mayonnaise and orange juice. Set aside.

3 Rinse shrimp and scallops; pat dry with paper towels. On four long metal skewers alternately thread shrimp and scallops. Grill for 5 to 8 minutes or until shrimp and scallops are opaque, turning frequently.

4 Meanwhile, arrange greens on four dinner plates. Top with fruit. Use a fork to push seafood from one skewer onto each salad. Spoon chutney mixture over salads.

Makes 4 servings

U.S. Per Serving: 295 calories, 36g carbohydrate, 28g protein, 5g fat, 3g fiber, 152mg cholesterol, 521mg sodium, 0g Omega-3
Canada Per Serving: 1236.57 kJ, 27.95g protein, 4.69g fat, 36.07g carbohydrate, 3.46g dietary fibre, 520.96mg sodium, 362.14mg potassium, 0.43g Omega-3

shrimp

peanut sauced shrimp & vegetables

Prep Time: 25 minutes
Cook Time: 2 minutes

12 oz. (340g) fresh or thawed shrimp, peeled and deveined
4 cups (.95l) water
1 tsp. (5ml) salt
½ cup (118ml) water
¼ cup (59ml) creamy peanut butter
¼ cup (59ml) apricot preserves
2 tbsp. (30ml) reduced-sodium soy sauce
2 tsp. (10ml) cornstarch
Dash ground red pepper
3 cups (710ml) thawed stir-fry vegetables
Hot cooked rice (optional)
Peanuts (optional)

1 Rinse shrimp; pat dry with paper towels. In a large saucepan bring 4 cups (.95 litres) of water and salt to a boil. Add shrimp. Return to a boil; reduce heat. Simmer, uncovered, for 1 to 4 minutes or until shrimp are opaque. Rinse under cold water. Drain.

2 In a large skillet stir together remaining ½ cup (118 millilitres) water, peanut butter, apricot preserves, soy sauce, cornstarch and red pepper. Bring to a boil; reduce heat. Cook and stir for 2 minutes.

3 Stir in vegetables and shrimp. Cook for 2 to 4 minutes or until heated through. Serve over rice and sprinkle with peanuts, if desired.

Makes 4 servings

U.S. Per Serving: 268 calories, 24g carbohydrate, 23g protein, 10g fat, 3g fiber, 129mg cholesterol, 1110mg sodium, 0g Omega-3
Canada Per Serving: 1123.08 kJ, 22.86g protein, 9.57g fat, 24.06g carbohydrate, 3.36g dietary fibre, 1110.10mg sodium, 188.97mg potassium, 0.42g Omega-3

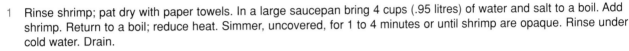

how to peel & devein shrimp

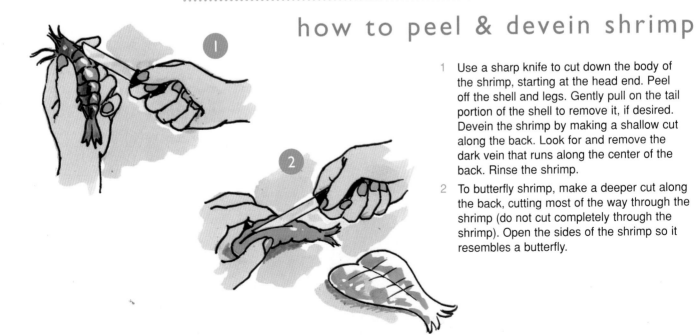

1 Use a sharp knife to cut down the body of the shrimp, starting at the head end. Peel off the shell and legs. Gently pull on the tail portion of the shell to remove it, if desired. Devein the shrimp by making a shallow cut along the back. Look for and remove the dark vein that runs along the center of the back. Rinse the shrimp.

2 To butterfly shrimp, make a deeper cut along the back, cutting most of the way through the shrimp (do not cut completely through the shrimp). Open the sides of the shrimp so it resembles a butterfly.

snapper

While there are more than 200 species of snapper, the most commonly harvested are red, yellowtail, mutton, gray or mangrove, lane and cubera snappers. Only one species may legally be called red snapper and it is in great demand. On the West Coast, snapper must be identified as Pacific red snapper to distinguish it from red snapper.

SOURCE: Snapper are found from North Carolina to Brazil. Most catches are by long-line fishermen in the Gulf of Mexico.

SELECTION & HANDLING: Snapper are available year-round, with the greatest supply during the summer months. Smaller snappers are sold whole or dressed, while larger snappers are often cut into steaks or fillets. Both small and large fish are sold fresh or frozen. Skin color is the key to identifying the species of snapper, so in almost all markets the skin is left on the fish.

FLAVOR: Mild but distinctive.

FLESH: Moderately firm with a fine flake.

PREPARATION: Snapper cook well with any technique, but they are especially suited to baking and broiling. Snapper is enhanced by the addition of delicate flavors such as dill weed or lime juice.

Prep Time: 20 minutes
Cook Time: 10 minutes

4 (5- to 6-oz./142 to 170g) red snapper fillets with skin, about ½ inch (1.3cm) thick
2 tsp. (10ml) thawed orange juice concentrate
2½ cups (591ml) finely chopped fresh pineapple
½ cup (118ml) chopped red bell pepper

1 medium jalapeño pepper, finely chopped*
4 tsp. (20ml) thawed orange juice concentrate
1 tbsp. (15ml) chopped fresh cilantro

1. Lightly coat the grill rack with nonstick cooking spray. Preheat the grill to medium.

2. Rinse fish; pat dry with paper towels. Brush fish with 2 teaspoons (30 millilitres) of the orange juice concentrate. Season with pepper. Set aside.

3. Tear one 36x18-inch (91x46-centimetre) piece of heavy foil. Fold in half to make an 18-inch (46-centimetre) square. Place pineapple, red pepper and jalapeño pepper in center. Drizzle with remaining 4 teaspoons (20 millilitres) orange juice concentrate. Toss to coat. Bring up opposite edges of foil; seal with a double fold. Fold remaining edges together to completely enclose food, leaving space for steam to expand.

4. Grill packet for 10 to 12 minutes or until hot. Place fish on the grill 5 minutes after starting packet, cooking for 5 to 7 minutes or until fish flakes with a fork (145°F/63°C), turning once.

5. Carefully open foil packet and sprinkle pineapple mixture with cilantro. Serve with fish.

Makes 4 servings

*Use caution when handling hot peppers. Wear disposable gloves or wash hands thoroughly with hot soapy water.

U.S. Per Serving: 209 calories, 17g carbohydrate, 30g protein, 2g fat, 2g fiber, 52mg cholesterol, 92mg sodium, 1g Omega-3
Canada Per Serving: 875.44 kJ, g 29.87protein, 2.39g fat, 16.80g carbohydrate, 1.71g dietary fibre, 92.42mg sodium, 801.79mg potassium, 0.51g Omega-3

red snapper baked in wine

Prep Time: 10 minutes
Cook Time: 30 minutes

1 (3-lb./1.36kg) fresh or thawed dressed whole red snapper
1 medium onion, thinly sliced
1 medium green bell pepper, thinly sliced
1 medium tomato, chopped

1 tsp. (5ml) dried thyme, crushed
1 tbsp. (15ml) olive oil
⅓ cup (79ml) dry white wine
Lemon wedges (optional)

1. Preheat oven to 400°F/204°C. Rinse fish; pat dry with paper towels. Layer onion, pepper and tomato in cavity of fish. Sprinkle with thyme.

2. Line 15x10x1-inch (25x38x2.5-centimetre) jelly-roll pan with foil. Place fish in pan. Brush with some oil. Drizzle wine over fish.

3. Bake for 15 minutes. Turn fish. Brush with remaining oil. Bake for 15 to 25 minutes more or until fish begins to flake with a fork (145°F/63°C). Serve with lemon wedges, if desired.

Makes 6 servings

U.S. Per Serving: 272 calories, 4g carbohydrate, 47g protein, 6g fat, 1g fiber, 84mg cholesterol, 149mg sodium, 1g Omega-3
Canada Per Serving: 1137.20 kJ, 47.11g protein, 5.52g fat, 3.98g carbohydrate, 1g dietary fibre, 148.54mg sodium, 1064.26mg potassium, 0.72g Omega-3

tilapia

Tilapia is also known as St. Peter's fish because many biblical scholars believe it to be the fish that St. Peter caught at the Red Sea. Other common names for tilapia include mouthbrooder and Nile perch.

SOURCE: A native of Africa, tilapia is farm-raised in tropical and temperate climates all over the world.

SELECTION & HANDLING: Tilapia is sold whole and as fresh or frozen fillets. The color of the meat varies, but pinkish to off-white is most common. If tilapia meat has a grayish hue or is dull, the fish is past its prime.

FLAVOR: Like all farm-raised fish, tilapia's flavor depends on the fish's diet and water quality. When fed controlled diets, tilapia have a consistently mild, slightly sweet flavor.

FLESH: Moderately firm with tender flakes.

PREPARATION: Tilapia is excellent baked, broiled, sautéed and grilled. Deep-frying may toughen it. Because it is so mild, tilapia is great for showcasing special flavors, such as garlic, dill or lime. It may be used in any recipe calling for flounder or snapper.

Prep Time: 15 minutes
Cook Time: 4 minutes

⅔ cup (158ml) seeded, chopped cucumber
½ cup (118ml) chopped radishes
2 tbsp. (30ml) tarragon vinegar
1 tsp. (5ml) olive oil
¼ tsp. (1ml) dried tarragon, crushed
Dash sugar
4 (6-oz./170g) fresh or thawed tilapia fillets, about ½ inch (1.3cm) thick
2 tbsp. (30ml) butter or margarine

1 In a medium bowl toss together cucumber, radishes, vinegar, oil, tarragon and sugar. Season with salt and pepper. Set aside.

2 Rinse fish; pat dry with paper towels. In a large skillet heat butter. Add tilapia. Cook for 4 to 6 minutes or until fish begins to flake with a fork (145°F/63°C), turning once.

3 Transfer fish to a warm platter. Spoon cucumber mixture on top.

Makes 4 servings

U.S. Per Serving: 234 calories, 3g carbohydrate, 32g protein, 11g fat, 0g fiber, 98mg cholesterol, 94mg sodium, 0g Omega-3
Canada Per Serving: 977.88 kJ, 31.72g protein, 11.03g fat, 2.73g carbohydrate, 0.39g dietary fibre, 93.92mg sodium, 68.05mg potassium, 0.01g Omega-3

tilapia Veracruz

Prep Time: 10 minutes
Cook Time: 6 minutes

1 (14½-oz./411g) can diced tomatoes with green chiles
2 tbsp. (30ml) sliced pimiento-stuffed green olives
1 tsp. (5ml) lemon juice
1 clove garlic, minced
4 (5-oz./142g) fresh or thawed tilapia fillets, about ½ inch (1.3cm) thick
2 tsp. (10ml) olive oil
Hot cooked rice (optional)

1 In a medium bowl stir together undrained tomatoes, olives, lemon juice and garlic. Set aside.

2 Rinse fish; pat dry with paper towels. Season tilapia with pepper.

3 In large skillet heat oil. Add fish. Cook for 3 minutes. Turn fish. Pour tomato mixture over fish. Cook for 2 to 5 minutes more or until fish begins to flake with a fork (145°F/63°C) and sauce slightly thickens. Serve with hot cooked rice, if desired.

Makes 4 servings

U.S. Per Serving: 195 calories, 6g carbohydrate, 28g protein, 6g fat, 2g fiber, 69mg cholesterol, 151mg sodium, 0g Omega-3
Canada Per Serving: 816.30 kJ, 27.88g protein, 6.47g fat, 5.53g carbohydrate, 1.60g dietary fibre, 150.56mg sodium, 201.93mg potassium, 0g Omega-3

trout

Trout describes a family of fish found primarily in freshwater lakes and streams, although some live in ocean waters. Common species of trout include rainbow, steelhead, brook, sea and lake.

SOURCE: Wild trout are caught in the cold-water lakes of the northern United States and Canada. Farm-raised trout come from many different countries.

SELECTION & HANDLING: Trout are sold fresh or frozen as whole fish, dressed fish, split fish or fillets. Some breaded and frozen fillets are marketed. Use fresh or thawed fish within 24 hours. With frozen fish avoid signs of freezer burn and signs of thawing and refreezing.

FLAVOR: Delicate.

FLESH: Moderately firm texture with colors that vary from white, to yellow-orange, to pink and to red.

PREPARATION: The traditional cookery method for trout is pan-frying. However, they are also good poached, baked, steamed, grilled or broiled. Stuffing a whole fish before baking works well.

Prep Time: 10 minutes
Cook Time: 8 minutes

⅓ cup (79ml) Italian seasoned fine dry bread crumbs
2 tbsp. (30ml) shredded Parmesan cheese
2 tbsp. (30ml) butter, softened
1 clove garlic, minced
1 tsp. (5ml) finely shredded lemon peel
2 tbsp. (30ml) pine nuts
4 (4- to 5-oz./113 to 142g) sea trout fillets

1   Preheat grill to medium. In a small bowl combine bread crumbs, Parmesan, butter, garlic and lemon peel. Stir in pine nuts.

2   Place fish on a greased grill rack over medium heat. Spoon crumb mixture on top of fish; spread slightly.

3   Grill, covered, for 5 minutes per ½-inch (1.3-centimetre) thickness or until fish flakes easily when tested with a fork.

Makes 4 servings

U.S. Per Serving: 243 calories, 7g carbohydrate, 22g protein, 14g fat, 1g fiber, 112mg cholesterol, 344mg sodium, 0g Omega-3
Canada Per Serving: 1016.16 kJ, 22.18g protein, 13.65g fat, 7.39g carbohydrate, 0.54g dietary fibre, 343.53mg sodium, 415.23mg potassium, 0.45g Omega-3

trout amandine

Prep Time: 10 minutes
Cook Time: 4 minutes

2 lb. (907g) fresh or thawed rainbow trout fillets, about ½ inch (1.3cm) thick
1 lemon, cut into 8 wedges
¼ cup (59ml) sliced almonds, toasted
¼ cup (59ml) chopped fresh parsley

1   Preheat the broiler. Lightly coat the rack of a broiler pan with nonstick cooking spray.

2   Rinse fish; pat dry with paper towels. Rub trout with lemon juice from 2 of the lemon wedges. Place fish on the broiler pan rack. Broil 4 to 5 inches (10 to 13 centimetres) from heat for 3 to 5 minutes or until fish almost flakes with a fork, turning once.

3   Sprinkle with almonds. Broil for 1 to 2 minutes more until fish flakes with a fork (145°F/63°C). Sprinkle with chopped parsley. Serve with remaining 6 lemon wedges.

Makes 6 servings

U.S. Per Serving: 236 calories, 3g carbohydrate, 33g protein, 10g fat, 1g fiber, 89mg cholesterol, 55mg sodium, 1g Omega-3
Canada Per Serving: 987.03 kJ, 32.69g protein, 10.24g fat, 2.87g carbohydrate, 1.40g dietary fibre, 54.90mg sodium, 750.68mg potassium, 1.49g Omega-3

tuna

Several species of tuna are sold, including yellowfin, bluefin, bigeye, tunny, bonito, ahi and albacore. Usually tuna have elongated silver bodies with bluish backs and large round eyes. They are fast swimmers and migrate long distances.

SOURCE: Found mainly in tropical and temperate waters, tuna may stray in the summer and autumn to northern latitudes. On the eastern shores of North America, yellowfin, bigeye and bluefin are harvested by longline.

SELECTION & HANDLING: Select tuna that is deep pink or red (not gray) and has a fresh smell. Avoid any with dry or brown spots or those with flesh that reflects rainbows. Steaks that are at least 1¼ inches (3.2cm) thick are less likely to dry out during cooking. Use within 1 or 2 days of purchase.

FLAVOR: Moderate.

FLESH: Very firm with a fairly fine flake. Ranges from pink to very deep red in color.

PREPARATION: Tuna is at its best grilled and is excellent poached or steamed. Because tuna dries out easily, avoid overcooking.

Prep Time: 5 minutes
Cook Time: 4 minutes

blackened tuna

2 tbsp. (30ml) dried Italian seasoning, crushed
1 tsp. (5ml) garlic powder
½ tsp. (2.5ml) onion powder
1 tsp. (5ml) olive oil
2 (4-oz./113g) fresh or thawed tuna steaks, about ½ inch (1.3cm) thick

1 In a small bowl combine Italian seasoning, garlic powder and onion powder.
Rinse fish; pat dry with paper towels. Rub herb mixture on both sides of fish steaks.

2 In a large skillet heat oil. Add tuna steaks. Cook for 4 to 6 minutes or until fish flakes
with a fork (145°F/63°C), turning once.

Makes 2 servings

U.S. Per Serving: 167 calories, 4g carbohydrate, 27g protein, 4g fat, 1g fiber, 50mg cholesterol, 46mg sodium, 0g Omega-3
Canada Per Serving: 696.76 kJ, 27.36g protein, 3.78g fat, 3.71g carbohydrate, 1.37g dietary fibre, 45.59mg sodium, 20.52mg potassium, 0g Omega-3

tuna with tropical salsa

Prep Time: 15 minutes
Cook Time: 10 minutes

½ cup (118ml) chopped guava, feijoa or kiwifruit
½ cup (118ml) chopped mango and/or papaya
½ cup (118ml) bite-size pieces fresh pineapple
¼ cup (59ml) finely chopped red bell pepper
2 to 3 tsp. (10 to 15ml) finely chopped jalapeño pepper*
1 tbsp. (15ml) fresh lime juice
4 (5- to 6-oz./142 to 170g) tuna steaks
2 tbsp. (30ml) pineapple juice

1 Preheat grill to medium. Combine guava, mango, pineapple,
red bell pepper, jalapeño pepper and lime juice. Cover and chill
until serving time.

2 Brush tuna steaks with pineapple juice.

3 Grill fish 5 minutes per ½-inch (1.3-centimetre) thickness, turning
once, or until fish flakes easily when tested with a fork (145°F/63°F).
Serve salsa over fish.

Makes 4 servings

*Use caution when handling hot peppers. Wear disposable gloves or
wash hands thoroughly with hot, soapy water.

U.S. Per Serving: 191 calories, 10g carbohydrate, 34g protein, 2g fat, 2g fiber,
63mg cholesterol, 56mg sodium, 0g Omega-3
Canada Per Serving: 797.78 kJ, 33.83g protein, 1.96g fat, 10.26g carbohydrate,
2.01g dietary fibre, 56.09mg sodium, 135.33mg potassium, 0.04g Omega-3

tuna

Prep Time: 15 minutes
Cook Time: 10 minutes

1¼ lb. (567g) fresh or thawed tuna steaks, about 1 inch (2.5cm) thick
3 Roma tomatoes, halved lengthwise
8 oz. (227g) asparagus spears, trimmed
2 tbsp. (30ml) bottled Caesar salad dressing
8 cups (2l) assorted torn greens
2 hard-cooked eggs, chopped or sliced
⅓ cup (79ml) pitted Nicoise olives or ripe olives
¾ cup (178ml) bottled Caesar salad dressing

1. Lightly coat the grill rack with nonstick cooking spray. Preheat the grill to medium.

2. Rinse fish; pat dry with paper towels. Cut into 6 serving-size pieces. Brush tuna steaks, tomato halves, and asparagus with 2 tablespoons (30 millilitres) of the salad dressing.

3. Grill tuna for 10 to 12 minutes or until fish flakes with a fork (145°F/63°C), turning once. Place tomato halves and asparagus on the grill 7 minutes after starting tuna, cooking for 3 to 4 minutes or until tomatoes are heated through and asparagus is tender.

4. Divide greens among 6 dinner plates. Arrange grilled tuna, tomatoes and asparagus on top of greens. Sprinkle with hard-cooked egg and olives. Drizzle with remaining ¾ cup (178 millilitres) salad dressing.

Makes 6 servings

U.S. Per Serving: 360 calories, 7g carbohydrate, 27g protein, 25g fat, 2g fiber, 114mg cholesterol, 558mg sodium, 0g Omega-3
Canada Per Serving: 1505.13 kJ, 27.25g protein, 25.05g fat, 6.91g carbohydrate, 1.53g dietary fibre, 558.49mg sodium, 89.82mg potassium, 0.01g Omega-3

ginger-marinated tuna steaks

Prep Time: 10 minutes
Marinate Time: 30 minutes
Cook Time: 10 minutes

4 (5- to 6-oz./142 to 170g) fresh or thawed tuna steaks, about 1 inch (2.5cm) thick
¼ cup (59ml) reduced-sodium soy sauce
2 tbsp. (30ml) dark sesame oil
2 tbsp. (30ml) rice vinegar
2 tbsp. (30ml) sliced green onion
1 tbsp. (15ml) grated gingerroot
1 clove garlic, minced

1. Rinse fish; pat dry with paper towels. Place tuna steaks in a plastic bag. Set bag in a shallow pan.

2. In a small bowl combine soy sauce, sesame oil, rice vinegar, green onion, gingerroot and garlic. Pour soy mixture over tuna; seal bag. Refrigerate for 30 minutes, turning bag occasionally.

3. Lightly coat the grill rack with nonstick cooking spray. Preheat the grill to medium. Drain tuna; discard marinade. Grill fish for 10 to 12 minutes or until fish flakes with a fork (145°F/63°C), turning once. Season with pepper, if desired.

Makes 4 servings

U.S. Per Serving: 232 calories, 3g carbohydrate, 35g protein, 9g fat, 0g fiber, 63mg cholesterol, 597mg sodium, 0g Omega-3
Canada Per Serving: 970.85 kJ, 35.09g protein, 8.73g fat, 3.07g carbohydrate, 0.12g dietary fibre, 597.34mg sodium, 18.11mg potassium, 0g Omega-3

Anadromous

Fish that live in oceans and migrate to fresh water rivers to spawn.

Aquaculture

Farm-raising aquatic plants and animals.

Bivalve

A mollusk, such as an oyster or clam, with a hinged two-part shell.

Black spot

Is a darkening of shrimp between the shell and tail, indicating deterioration. If present, do not purchase.

Bleeding

Cutting an artery of a fish behind the gills. It improves the condition and shelf-life of the fish.

Boned

All major bones have been removed.

Boneless fillet

Boneless pieces cut from the sides of the fish.

Bottomfish

Fish that live on the bottom of rivers, oceans, etc.

Breading

Flour, cornmeal, cracker crumbs or other ingredients used to coat seafood. Often applied prior to frying.

Butterfly

A technique for cutting fish or shrimp that cuts almost (but not quite) through the fish or shrimp, then the halves are opened to resemble a butterfly shape. A butterflied fish fillet is cut from both sides of the fish with the two pieces joined by a piece of skin. A butterflied shrimp is peeled and deveined, then cut from the back most of the way through.

Cakes

Patties made from seafood and other ingredients such as vegetables, seasonings and flour or cracker crumbs. They are usually sautéed or baked.

Calamari

Italian word for squid.

Carapace

The protective covering forming the upper body cover of a crab.

Caviar

Sieved and lightly salted fish eggs. Often served as an appetizer.

Cluster

A group of legs, a claw and the shoulder area from one side of a crab. Sometimes called a section.

Cold smoked

Seafood smoked around 80°F/27°C for long periods of time.

Counts

The number of shrimp or scallops per pound.

Crusher claw

The larger claw on American or Maine lobsters.

Crustacean

Shellfish with joined appendages and hard shells, including shrimp, lobster, crayfish and crabs.

Devein

To remove the dark vein (digestive tract) of shrimp, lobster or other crustaceans.

Dorsal

The top of a fish.

Double fillets

Butterflied fillets. The fillets from both sides of a fish joined by a small piece of skin.

Drawn

A gutted fish with the head and fins intact.

Dressed

A gutted and scaled fish with the gills removed. Often the fins are also removed.

Eviscerated

Gutted.

Fillets

Portions cut from the sides of a fish.

Flat fish

Species of fish with flat compressed bodies. Both eyes are on the top of the fish. They swim on one side only, looking like a platter.

Freezer burn

A loss of moisture and flavor in frozen food, resulting from improper packaging or handling. A dry surface and white or gray spots indicate freezer burn.

Fresh

Product that is raw and has never been frozen or heated.

Gaping

The separation of meat in a fish fillet or an opened shell of a live shellfish.

Gutted

Completely eviscerated.

H & G

Headed and gutted.

Hot smoked

Seafood smoked at gradually increasing temperatures up to 180°F/82°C.

IQF

Individually quick frozen.

J-Cut

A method of removing pinbones.

Mollusks

Soft-bodied and usually hard-shelled animals, including snails, clams, oysters, octopus and squid.

Molting

The process during which a crustacean sheds its shell to permit growth.

Omega-3 fatty acids

Polyunsaturated fats, found primarily in seafood, that may reduce the risks for cardiovascular disease.

P & D

Peeled and deveined.

Pan-dressed fish

Gutted and scaled fish with the head and fins removed. Often the tail is trimmed.

Pasteurization

A heating process to kill bacteria but not hot enough to cook food.

Pinbones

A strip of small bones found near the center of many fillets.

Prawn

A term used to describe very large shrimp. It is also the name for crustaceans resembling small lobsters and fresh water shrimp.

PTO

Peeled, tail-on shrimp.

PUD

Peeled, undeveined shrimp.

Red tide

A reddish discoloration of coastal waters due to concentrations of toxic algae.

Round fish

Whole, ungutted fish.

Seafood

All marine fish, crustaceans or mollusks harvested for human consumption.

Shelf life

The expected length of time that food will remain in high-quality condition under normal storage conditions.

Smoked

The process of curing food by exposing it to smoke produced from slowly burning wood or coals.

Steak

A crosscut slice cut from a whole dressed fish.

Tail

The thin tapered end of a fish. Or, the meaty tapered end of a lobster or shrimp.

Trimmed

Fish with the fins and tail removed.

V-cut

A cut made by cutting along both sides of the pinbone strip to remove the pinbones.

Vein

The intestinal tract of shrimp or lobsters.

Viscera

Internal organs.

index

A

Almond & Mushroom
   Topped Perch   59
Amandine, Trout   87
Appetizers: 39, 51, 69
Avocado Salsa, Shrimp
   Tacos with   75

B

Backyard Clambake   25
Baked Orange Roughy with Dill   61
Baking   15
Barbecued Grouper   43
Beer-Steamed Blue Crab   33
Blackened Grouper   43
Blackened Tuna   89
Blue Crab, Beer Steamed   33
Broiled Halibut with
   Tomato & Dill   49
Broiling   15
Buying fish   9
Buying seafood   9
Buying shellfish   9

C

Catfish   7, 8, 20-23
Catfish Fillets with Cornbread
   Stuffing   23
Catfish with Corn Relish   21
Catfish with Lemon Pepper   23
Catfish with Mustard Sauce   21
Cholesterol   7
Citrus Ginger Scallops   71
Citrus Haddock   47
Citrus Poached Orange
   Roughy   63
Citrus Sauce, Orange Roughy
   with Herbed   61
Clam Chowder, Manhattan   27
Clambake, Backyard   25
Clams   7, 8, 24-27
Clams in White Wine Broth   25
Cleaning   10
Cleaning fish   12
Coal temperature   17
Cod   7, 8, 28-31
Cod á la French Country   31
Cod, Cucumber-Topped   29
Cod, Milk Poached   31
Cod with Tomato Pesto   29
Cooking fish   14
Cooking seafood   11

Corn Relish, Catfish with   21
Cornbread Stuffing, Catfish
   Fillets with   23
Crab   8, 32-39
Crab & Tarragon Pasta, Snow   35
Crab Étouffée   37
Crab legs   35, 37
Crab Quesadillas with Papaya
   Sauce   39
Crab Royale, King   35
Crabcakes with Herb Sauce   33
Cracking crab   39
Cracking lobster   53
Creamy Tomato-Topped
   Flounder   41
Cucumber Relish, Tilapia with   85
Cucumber-Topped Cod   29

D

Defrosting seafood   11
Deveining shrimp   81
Direct heat grilling   16

E

Environmental concerns   13
Étouffée, Crab   37

F

Fat   5, 7
Filleting fish   12
Fish farming   13
Flavor descriptions   8
Flounder   7, 8, 40-41
Flounder, Creamy
   Tomato-Topped   41
Flounder, Lemon & Parsley   41
Food safety   10, 13
Forms of fish   12
Foreword   2
Freshness   9

G

Ginger-Marinated Tuna Steaks   91
Gingered Teriyaki Sauce,
   Salmon & Pineapple with   65
Glossary   92-93
Grilled Haddock with
   Orange-Chili Rub   45
Grilled Lemon-Butter Lobster   53
Grilled Mackerel, Spicy   55
Grilled Mahi Mahi   57
Grilled Tuna Nicoise Salad   91

Grilling   16-17
Grouper   7, 8, 42-43
Grouper, Barbecued   43
Grouper, Blackened   43

H

Haddock   7, 8, 44-47
Haddock, Citrus   47
Haddock Dilly   45
Haddock with
   Orange-Chili Rub, Grilled   45
Haddock with Spicy Shrimp
   Sauce   47
Halibut   7, 8, 48-49
Halibut with Tomato &
   Dill, Broiled   49
Health benefits   4-6
Herb Sauce, Crabcakes with   33
Herbed Citrus Sauce,
   Orange Roughy with   61
Honey & Mustard
   Halibut Skewers   49
Horseradish Sauce, Salmon with
   Creamy   69
How much seafood to buy   9
How to crack a cooked
   hard-shell crab   39
How to crack a cooked lobster   53
How to peel & devein shrimp   81
How to shuck a clam   27

I

Indirect heat grilling   16
Italian Crumb Topping,
   Sea Trout with   87

K

Kabobs   49, 75
Kabobs, Shrimp & Vegetable   75
King Crab Royale   35

L

Lemon & Parsley Flounder   41
Lemon-Butter Lobster, Grilled   53
Lemon Pepper, Catfish with   23
Lime & Tomato Mahi Mahi   57
Lime Butter, Lobster Tails with   51
Lobster   7, 8, 50-53
Lobster Cocktail   51
Lobster, Grilled Lemon-Butter   53
Lobster tails   51
Lobster Tails with Lime Butter   51

M

Mackerel   7, 8, 54-55
Mackerel Cayman   55
Mackerel, Spicy Grilled   55
Mahi mahi   8, 56-57
Mahi Mahi, Grilled   57
Mahi Mahi, Lime & Tomato   57
Manhattan Clam Chowder   27
Marinated Tuna Steaks, Ginger   91
Methyl mercury   13
Microwave cooking   15
Milk Poached Cod   31
Minerals   4
Mint & Mustard Sauced Salmon   67
Mushroom Topped Perch,
    Almond &   59
Mustard Halibut Skewers,
    Honey &   49
Mustard Sauce, Catfish with   21
Mustard Sauced Salmon, Mint &   67

N

Nutrition chart   7

O

Ocean perch   7, 8, 58-59
Ocean Perch with Pine Nuts   59
Omega-3 fatty acids   2, 5-6
Orange-Chili Rub, Grilled
    Haddock with   45
Orange roughy   7, 8, 60-63
Orange Roughy Baked in Wine   63
Orange Roughy, Citrus Poached   63
Orange Roughy with Dill, Baked   61
Orange Roughy with Herbed
    Citrus Sauce   61
Oysters   7, 8

P

Pan-frying   15
Papaya Sauce, Crab Quesadillas
    with   39
Peanut Sauced Shrimp &
    Vegetables   81
Peeling shrimp   81
Perch, Almond & Mushroom Topped   59
Pesto, Squash & Shrimp with   79
Pine Nuts, Ocean Perch with   59
Poached Cod, Milk   31
Poaching   15
Pollock   7, 8

Q

Quesadillas with Papaya Sauce,
    Crab   39

R

Raw seafood   13
Red Snapper Baked in Wine   83
Refrigerating seafood   11

S

Salad, Grilled Tuna Nicoise   91
Salad, Surimi Crab   37
Salad with Mango Dressing,
    Shrimp & Scallop   79
Salmon   7, 8, 64-69
Salmon & Pineapple with
    Gingered Teriyaki Sauce   65
Salmon, Mint & Mustard Sauced   67
Salmon Spread, Smoked   69
Salmon with Creamy
    Horseradish Sauce   69
Salmon with Tomatoes & Chives   65
Salmon with Tropical Salsa   67
Sautéing   15
Scallop Salad with Mango
    Dressing, Shrimp &   79
Scallops   7, 8, 70-71
Scallops, Citrus Ginger   71
Scallops with Thyme & Veggies   71
Sea bass   8, 72-73
Sea Bass, Smoked   73
Sea Bass with Ginger   73
Sea Trout with Italian Crumb
    Topping   87
Seafood Bisque   77
Seafood's contribution to
    healthy eating   4
Seasoning seafood   17
Shrimp   7, 8, 47, 74-81
Shrimp & Scallop Salad with
    Mango Dressing   79
Shrimp & Vegetable Kabobs   75
Shrimp & Vegetables, Peanut
    Sauced   81
Shrimp Paella   77
Shrimp Sauce, Haddock with Spicy   47
Shrimp Tacos with Avocado Salsa   75
Shrimp with Pesto, Squash &   79
Shucking Clams   27
Smoked Salmon Spread   69
Smoked Sea Bass   73

Smoking seafood   17
Snapper   7, 8, 82-83
Snapper Baked in Wine, Red   83
Snapper with Warm Pineapple
    Salsa   83
Snow Crab & Tarragon Pasta   35
Sole   7, 8
Soups   25, 27, 77
Spicy Grilled Mackerel   55
Spicy Shrimp Sauce,
    Haddock with   47
Squash & Shrimp with Pesto   79
Starting charcoal   17
Starting gas grill   17
Steamed Blue Crab, Beer   33
Steaming   15
Storing seafood   10-11
Suggested internal cooking
    temperatures   11
Surimi Crab Salad   37

T

Tacos with Avocado Salsa,
    Shrimp   75
10-minute rule   14
Teriyaki Sauce, Salmon &
    Pineapple with Gingered   65
Thyme & Veggies, Scallops with   71
Tilapia   7, 8, 84-85
Tilapia Veracruz   85
Tilapia with Cucumber Relish   85
Tomato Pesto, Cod with   29
Tomatoes & Chives, Salmon with   65
Tropical Salsa, Salmon with   67
Tropical Salsa, Tuna with   89
Trout   7, 8, 86-87
Trout Amandine   87
Tuna   7, 8, 88-91
Tuna, Blackened   89
Tuna Nicoise Salad, Grilled   91
Tuna Steaks, Ginger-Marinated   91
Tuna with Tropical Salsa   89

V

Vegetable Kabobs, Shrimp &   75
Vitamins in seafood   4-5

W

Warm Pineapple Salsa,
    Snapper with   83
White Wine Broth, Clams in   25
Whiting   7, 8